Migrations and Home:
The Elements of Place

Migrations and Home: The Elements of Place
Edited by Simon Richard Wilson
Foreword by Joel Berger

Published by NatureCulture LLC
www.nature-culture.net   www.writingtheland.org

ISBN: 978-1-960293-00-8
Library of Congress Control Number: 2023942483

Cover Artwork: *Hummingbird* by Martin Bridge
www.thebridgebrothers.com
Cover design: Lis McLoughlin and Christopher Gendron
Interior book design: Lis McLoughlin

Related Volumes:
From Root to Seed: Black, Brown, and Indigenous Poets Write the Northeast edited
by Samaa Abdurraqib (2023)
Writing the Land: Streamlines (2023)
Writing the Land: Channels (2023)
Writing the Land: Currents (2023)
Writing the Land: Foodways and Social Justice (2022)
Writing the Land: Windblown I (2022)
Writing the Land: Windblown II (2022)
Writing the Land: Maine (2022)
LandTrust poems by Katherine Hagopian Berry (2022)

For more information: www.nature-culture.net

Migrations and Home:
The Elements of Place

Edited by Simon Richard Wilson
Foreword by Joel Berger

Published by
NatureCulture LLC
Northfield, MA

Foreword: Who We Are
Connections by a Migrations Scientist

As a scientist who studies migration, I frequently offer public lectures. I want to offer conservation outcomes. I want to inspire. Most frequently, the purity of unadulterated science fails. A human face and heart are needed.

So I do not tout the data on the spectacular journeys of Monarch butterflies. I do not discuss the movement of humpback whales. I fail to offer up the boring minutia about millions of migrating crabs. Instead, I try to connect. And this is precisely what this anthology does too. It connects.

Migrations and Home: The Elements of Place offers a fascinating and emotionally positive portal to the world of movement— movement of our hearts and spirits through the lens of refuge and conservation. Seasons pass. Animal pass. Plants jump and the wind churns. We live, we breathe, and we reshape the planet. Within the pages we find refuge and calm. Encounters. Reflections grow deep. And challenges arise from growth of our planet from a home to few human souls to that of eight billion. This is a volume about splendor and quiet, about stars, and sun, and earth, about water and rocks, and about the species that rise or sink in this complex milieu. We can imagine the past when plants and animals moved around the planet – in the air, in the oceans, and across unfettered landscapes.

This is not the dry, empirical view of a scientist; nor is it a compendium of actionable conversation. Instead, deep, global poetic justice and injustice are intertwined in the poems' tendrils. In *Migrations and Home* we see through the poets' eyes images of movement across the Earth in all its hope and intrigue. The poetry within fascinates, shapes, and inspires. It challenges us to think, to consider our past, and our future. *Migrations and Home* is a beautiful reflection of who we are.

—Dr. Joel Berger, Chair of Wildlife Conservation, Colorado State University; Senior Scientist of the Wildlife Conservation Society; and author of *Extreme Conservation: Life at the Edges of the World*
June 2023

Photo: Monarch Butterfly by Marty Espinola

Preface: Mapping and Meaning

The volume you hold in your hand is, as its title suggests, an extended meditation on the themes of migrations and home. As the poetry (and a little prose) collected here make quite clear, these twinned and intwined terms are opposites only at first glance. If migration may be driven by yearning or brute necessity, so, too, is home. Home is not a static or stubbornly permanent place. It is a constantly transforming gesture towards a type of happiness and rootedness which is as much metaphysical as physical. It is a model, or occasionally perhaps merely a counterfeit, of our true home, which may always seem elsewhere. Home is a place of constant migrations. Migrations may be our home.

Migrants may cover great distances, leaving their home searching for home. They may cross political, personal, environmental boundaries; find new landscapes; and encounter new land, new spaces, new possibilities and presences. At some cost, old realities may be left behind. Equally they may journey further into aspects of themselves, crossing interior boundaries; discovering new landscapes of the soul; and encountering new imaginative, spiritual, intellectual or emotional possibilities, perils and presences. These interior journeys, too, may lead to a new but always provisional sense of home: in the heart, in the spirit, in the consciousness. Heart is where the home is: but where is it?

These migrations – these wanderings - occur simultaneously, the outer lives of the land and the wanderer informing their inner lives, and vice versa, in an intricate and endless web of reciprocal relations, like a richly interwoven tapestry or Celtic knot.

"May this poem be a portal/or a map" wishes (prays?) Lynne Shapiro in the opening piece of the collection. A portal to what, a map of what? The poem – and all the poetry here – may show us, but still it is up to us to explore, in the manifold ways which seem fit to us, the new land which may (or may not) lie before us. Sonia Overall, in the title of her poem, takes us on *three walks without maps*: mapless perhaps, but still they are walks, and we may choose to trust the poet even as we stray.

Our wayward wanderings may lead to the realisation that we are infinite and everything and everywhere, as in Yuan Hongri's *My Heaven is Inside My Body*, and so any movement is just an illusion. That, too, however, may just be a moment, provisional and precarious like the "Transformation into peace" in Elaine Reardon's *Cassidy's Pub*. Always already we are captured by yearning for migration and home, as happens to Yehudit Silverman in *The Calling*. When that occurs, yearning and calling meet in an endless spiralling dance, "urging you to turn/from your scavenging on earth/toward the mystery of flight" (Cynthia Anderson, *Möbius*). Though what is earthbound and what is mystery may be a matter of perspective: "*Still circling, nearly-finishing, never resting/*say the bees/*I'll see you on the other side of the rose/*says each rose" (Katherine Pierpoint, *Foxglove, or 'snoxum'*).

The words of this vagrant preface are certainly no map. Readers will notice, however, that we have divided the poems into short sections or sequences, marked by a mysterious glyph, which is in fact an alchemical symbol. Alchemy, with its yearning for change, mapped in careful stages but rarely if ever reaching its end, seems an appropriate guide (which in truth is no guide at all) to migrations and home. We have deliberately left unexplained the symbols themselves and their relation to the sections they mark. Readers may decide to explore them, and map out their own meanings. The book may thus generate as many maps as there are readers, becoming a seemingly endless source of migrations and an infinity of homes.

—*Simon Richard Wilson*
8 June, 2023
Bridge, England

MIGRATIONS AND HOME:
THE ELEMENTS OF PLACE

☿

🜁 △ 🜄 ▽

♀

♈

♉

ᛟ

For Lise, who is at Home.

Crossings
by Lynne Shapiro

I.

May this poem be a portal
or a map,

breadcrumbs, a way out,
a way back.

In Santa Lucia, near Vejer, the scarlet
hibiscus unfurls with first light,

folds like an umbrella with setting sun.
Aperture, unseen, remembered,

like the garden, the first garden —
the garden within.

Lately, the lyric is absent.
Poetry feels too pretty, like ballet,

seems beside the point, too too clever,
overwrought.

Now I too am vanished between cupboard and sink, lost
in quarantine to sanitizing and serving.

To keep peace, I try on the rhythm of others
but that doesn't stop the unintended trampling of toes.

Then I remember to remember.

Lynne, look to the sky.
There are birds, lots of them.
Lots of them.
Migrating.

I'm in the hibiscus garden.
I hear Pol's voice and look up.

It's the autumnal flight of storks,
the world without end.

Throngs pass and pass proudly. Stretches of joyous
configurations go on and on without pause.

When the carpet of birds begins to thin,
the storks swirl round and round

waiting for the last bird, who searches for possible stragglers
before they move on into the paleness beyond sight.

The pageantry gone, I'm exhausted and ache
from the affliction of having seen too much beauty.

Stendhal syndrome, like swallowing too much air.
I lay on the grass arms outstretched,

try on the fanfare of the southbound muster, join
Ciconia ciconia's endless ribbon,

and relive the raucous freedom of convergence
from all points north

in congregation for the great migration over
the Strait of Gibraltar — just a few miles away,

each bird having birthed or having been born
into this ecstatic crossing.

Their journey a reverse of mine.
I ferried from Tangier to Tarifa

To the hibiscus garden's house on a floating portal
across the Strait amidst immigrant families

whose tongues spoke every possibility, who converged
from various lands like the storks.

My ears, whirling pistils of receptivity
heard angelic voices as I merged,

and recalled how I merged, with that abundant phalanx
of boundless life —

benediction.

II.

The beauty of humanity and birds, vanished
over coffee in my kitchen.

The headline read *Bodies Wash Ashore.*
Thousands of migrants lost in crossing from Africa.

The photo showed a small milk-blue boat,
weathered, sand-filled, abandoned

by the shore, Vejer de la Frontera, Spain.
I was there.

On that beach,
waiting for sunrise.

Twinkling lights across dark waters
on both sides of the Strait.

A record year for migrant drownings.
I had no idea the crossing dangerous,

after all, my ferry ride was untroubled.
My travels, born of curiosity

and connection —
friends, djellaba buttons, and storks.

I didn't imagine how desperate a 27-year old
mechanic from Tangier might be,

or that there were hundreds
like him, young and hungry; their travels travails.

Many never *make it to Spain alive.*
I didn't know of Martin Zamora,

mortuary owner, who took it upon himself to repatriate
broken bodies, some wasting away at sea for months;

some nameless for years,
some nameless still.

The clothes are often the only clues.
No way out. One way back.

No breadcrumbs to a better life.
Bitter-sweet homecoming.

The tourist in the garden
sees only flowers.

I wrote these lines about the visitor,
the ease with which one overlooks

the whole, misses subtleties,
the varieties of green.

I read those lines differently today; see myself
as the tourist who yearned *only for the easy beauty.*

I didn't close my eyes to the truth —
but I didn't question what else might be true.

In the end, beauty remains;
it lives in Mr. Zamora —

the Body Collector of Algeciras,
and now his son who helps him,

their sense of duty,
and the final act of benediction

they bestow on those who die at sea
with fists-full of faith.

N.B. *Part I first published: Shapiro, Lynne.* To Set Right, *2022, WordTech* *Editions*

Love Song for Mexico
by Dana Maya

You are the clouds

And I am the mountain

I am the streetdog

And you are the *calavera*

You are the skeleton

And I am the desert

You are the dancer

And I am the rain

I am the feathers

And you are the rattle

You are the clouds

And I am the corn

I am the jaguar

And you are the *aguila*

I am the dream

And you are the dragon

You are the boy

And I am his dream

I am the devil

And you are the donkey

You are the fire

And also the smoke

I am the cactus

And we are the desert

You are my braids

And I am your face

Your mamá is the *bruja*

And I am her gaze

I am the false god and

You are the *virgen*

I am the fur

And you are the feathers

You are the *selva*

And I am your flowers

I am the nest

And you are my beak

I am the *palma*

And you are its *coco*

I am the fingers

And you are my palm

You are mi *reyna*

And I am the queen

You are the mask

And also the wrestler

I am the gate

And you are the falling

                          god

You are the sun

And I am the flight

I am the sky

And you are the footprints

Mi abuela is the stone

And yours is the cross

I am the *piñata*

And you are the stick

I am the blindfold

And you are the spin

I am the *dulces*

And you are the song

You are the *¡TRAS!*

And I am the *¡SAS!*

You are the *cuerda*

And I am the pull

I am the hand

And you are the rooster

I am the drunk

And you are my drink

This is the nightmare

But also the dream

The men are the *migra*

And we are the boy

You are the *nopal*

And I am the slingshot

We are the *espina*

And also the toy

We are the cactus

And also the slingshot

I am the cactus

And you are its joy

Infernal Platoons
by Gwyn R. C. Moses

Trees
Intertwine
Swing
Rhythmically
Intermingle
Knot calamity
Interconnect
One strand of lavender
Intersect
Topples a full green branch
Interpenetrate
It's spring!
Indescribable
Tis season for revival!

Leaves which dare
Pay a price for winter's stay
Strangle bark
Witness slavish land
Darkened pistils
Amid virtuous leaves
Create veils
Silhouettes mat openings of flowering
As bullet ridden soldiers
Nail pinned bodies
Fall like collapsing beams

Under metallic moonlight
Shadows on the riverbank
Drag fluttering leaves
Condemn bowing
Shame regrets
Pools of marsh
Suck in blue eyed hibiscus
Swollen

Misplaced
Hope is due
To show up only as a surrender

Surrender to the colors the sun set
Upon ocean waters blue
Brown soil of Mother Earth
Mustard and purple water lilies
Mimicking pigments of combined skin
Immerse same disgrace
Freedom is a beggar
Ripples and fight
Spools like a river
Drowning sacrifice

Once strong and fervent
Hearts pounded like a last trumpet
On a glorious day
Calling unto the skies
Wherein soldiers' tears welled up
Forever to bring forth rain
After a dry season
To scorch like fire

Weeping for humankind
Kind human
Whose countenance will rise up
From the waters
To be lifted
Into the skies
As such are cunning angels
Tis such repeated demise of war

three walks without maps
by Sonia Overall

tongue

The city is tacky-edged. Circuit this perimeter of glue, licked by the tongue of river.

Water runs fast beyond the weir. Follow paths of bark chip banked by split logs, twisting between trees. Wait for a dog walker to pass, fetid black plastic bag swinging from the knot. Look away. Examine the tree-rings of a supine trunk. Listen for the road against the roar of river. Metallic car-flashes on the bridge are trout, jumping midstream.

Pass the cog-and-bolt of the weir gate. See it for what it is: a giant scold's bridle for silencing riversong.

nails

Walk each finger on the spread hands of a town. Hidden histories snag under the grimy fingernails. That's where you want to be. That's what never fails to draw you.

ghosts

Scout the gravel arc before the gates of building site, scoured by traction marks. Close your eyes and listen for the faint hiss of ghosts beyond, buried in builders' spoil.

Find them everywhere you walk: massing beneath limbs of heart-shaped foliage; pressing against rust-flecked iron railings. Rustling leaf litter, broken branches, silt, flung packages.
Trapped. Pathless.

Keep out signs. Rusted padlocks.

Valerian sways in defiant mulberry sprays.

North Atlantic Fracture Zones
by Linda Buckmaster

Under the North Atlantic's deep waters, a landscape lies,
a geography of fracture zones in the sea bed unseen
by emigrants from the Highlands riding rough seas
to the unknowns of Nova Scotia and Newfoundland.
Where they'll work, "na better 'n slaves," on other boats
steaming from the Grand Banks or down from the Labrador
to the land crew of women and children toiling on the flakes,
all for the making of salt cod. Barrels of it,
the best grade hauled overseas to Europe
or the cheapest to the Indies to feed black slaves
owned by Glasgow merchants getting fat on sugar.

Aye, many fractures there are.
In the North, the Charlie-Gibbs Fracture Zone,
and farther south the Oceanographer Fracture,
the Atlantis, the Kane, the Vema, the Doldrums.
There is the goodbye to the land of ancestors fracture.
Your mum dying while at sea fracture. The lash
of the overseer's whip fracturing flesh from bone.
The hand caught between dory and schooner
offloading fish. The hauling block
upside the back of the head on a rogue wave.
The machete lopping off an arm caught in the sugar mill.
The fractures of a life, lives, lost to struggle and short pay.

And running north and south down
the middle of the ocean for ten thousand miles,
the great Mid-Atlantic Ridge crosses
the fractures that bind
Europe and North America,
Africa and Indies,
East of, West of,
Before, after.

The Headland
by Linda Buckmaster
East Coast, Newfoundland, present day

Always poor people, but they made a living. Land-poor, you might say.
His grandfather had two hundred acres along the headland that he got
from his grandfather. Wasn't much use for it—just tuckamore and berry
barrens, shore too high to bring a boat in and no beach to speak of for
the cod drying flakes.

Yes, you could, and did, berry in season, plenty of those: bakeapple,
raspberry, blueberry, kinnikinnick. No money in that, though. And
anybody has the right to pick berry land. The grandson can see the
pickers even now leaning like ladders against the hill's pitch.

So a wee house in town it was and the grandfather working day boats,
and the grandmother making the salt fish with the other women on the
beach and afterwards setting a solid meal in front of him. Some grand
times, for a while.

It's all the grandson's now. He always loved the headland's long wild views
of the Atlantic stretching like a possibility. His grandfather showed him
how set a trapline for rabbits out there in the winter to keep the family
fed. Maybe there'd be a fox or marten pelt to send up to St. John's for
money in your pocket to buy candy for you and your mates. Sometimes,
the two of them snow-shoed to the shabby tilt a mile in to hunt deer,
the wind at night beating around outside and the wolves howling and
the smoke of the grandfather's pipe patrolling the shack and holding it
safe and cozy. It was always "them two" in those days—grandfather and
grandson.

But still the land not of much use and the fish mostly done now. A
girlfriend and a baby, so he goes out west with the rest of them to the
Alberta oil fields: three weeks on, three weeks off. Steady pay and good
money. New roof on the old place and another room for the babe. (How
did all of them live in those two rooms back then? He never questioned
before.)

Then the accident. "Not your fault," his mates say. "Could've been any one of us." The company pays to fly him home, the Halifax airport at midnight for the connection and no one to have a beer with for the wait. "Never be the same," they say after the surgery. "Better get another line of work."

So now there's nothing else for it but to sell lots on the headland—"long, narrow lots," they say, "is the smart money." That way, those from St. John's or Ontario can have a road at one end and their own waterfront on the other.

The grandson turns his back to the wind to roll a cigarette. Yes, that's the right thing to do, he thinks as he takes his first drag. Family to mind— sell lots. Yes, that's the only thing to do. He steps around the corner into the wind and sees the Atlantic, cold and green, snapping with white caps, stretching out before him as it always has, except now it feels like a rebuke.

subterranean trees
by Robin Lily Goldberg

moonlight went missing
on the voyage
from human to hidden,

besamim boxes went overboard,

separating
       cinnamon mothers
       from chamomile maidens,

splicing
       sweet spinal strands
       into numerical mysteries.

rebuilding bridges
between homelands
       demands
alphabetizing
       Indigenous
       before
       digital,

reclaiming our roots
requires
sailing through soil,
wearing mismatched socks,
       and breathing our selves
       back into our cells.

Heat
by W. Luther Jett

In that dry season
the hillcrest shimmered
under yellow skies.

If we could reach
the river, there the willows
might shelter us.

Between the spur
and the cool banks
sharp stones baked.

A distant flag
was a wound ripped
across the horizon.

A child's balloon
ignited mid-air —
birds with wings of flame.

Under the overhang
of green root, minnows
darted unaware.

Five Landays
by W. Luther Jett

Show me a nation without hope
and I will show you a land without poets.

Even the smallest flower
can cause a desert to bloom.

Two sounds shake the earth —
Guns of war. Trill of one lone sparrow.

Don't weave a shroud of your tears.
Spin them into a ladder.

Long after dust covers everything
water will still find the sea.

— For the women of Afghanistan

Tectonic
by Meg Weston

> 1. *relating to the structure of the earth's crust and the large scale processes which take place within it.*
> 2. *a change or development very significant or considerable.*

1.

I've been obsessed since I was thirteen with a single image of the eruption of Surtsey off the coast of Iceland. A tongue of lava pushes back the waves, an island appears from nowhere. It rises along a fault line that intersects the earth like a seam sewn by a seamstress with a shaky hand, jutting this way and that, bisecting the globe into plates that collide against one another or rip open the ocean floor to spill blood and tear the earth apart beneath the sea. The plates move at the speed your fingernails grow, slowly, inexorably tearing Iceland in two, one side moving towards Europe, the other drifting over to North America.

2.

I'm sheltered-in for months as a pandemic spreads across the globe, the world, it seems, erupts in protest over centuries of subjugation, the flora and fauna spiral towards extinction. I look out from windows that I've spent the past month washing. My world appears bubble-wrapped in endless Amazon packaging stretched around the fenced-in yard. Each morning rose-colored light dances with the shadows on my closet doors. Giant heads of peonies nod into bloom, a robin steals the worms from our first vegetable garden, newly planted. The evening news shouts from the large-screen TV—this is what's happening—forces me to look, until I shut it off and go to bed. At night the virus slips past my dreamcatcher and enters my dreams. "You are going to die," the doctor tells me, then asks "How do you feel about that?" I answer, "I am OK with death. Just not today."

My cocoon of beauty holds still while the earth shifts. Imperceptible. Momentous.

The Stone Monologues
by Alyson Hallett

1

The quest is to understand myself not as a single
thing, a single point, but rather a constellation, a
layered interruption in time comprising everyone
and everything I encounter.

2

When I said I wanted to leave home my mother
wept. I have never seen such a storm on the
mountain and I feared she would not let me go.
The tears she cried froze around me and I was
swaddled in ice for a thousand years.

I rode the back of the Earth until the sun
turned my horse into water.

It broke my mother's heart to see me leave and
that breaking made my journey possible.

3

When I arrived in the foreign land I knew no-one.
All I had to offer were songs and stories from my
mother-land. For a long time the people around
me could not understand what I was saying. They
thought their world and their ways were the only
ones and feared I might want to change them.

Exchange, I said, *that is what I want.*

4

Everything I have come to understand as being
one way is no longer that way. The straight line
becomes a curve, the contradiction becomes
coherent, poverty becomes wealth. This is the
great law of reversal my ancestors spoke of. It is

essentially expansive, essentially ignorant of
boundary, essentially counter to almost
everything we have come to believe.

Why, under reversal's banner even god has
descended from a heaven in the sky to live
as a worm in the earth.

5
One day men came. They dug metal stakes into the
ground around me and joined them with a rope.

But the rope that separates is also the rope that joins -

Particles of myself ride the wind into the homes
and hands of strangers. Rain washes me into earth
and the earth's fast running rivers. I record the
touch of a leaf, step of fly, scud of clouds. I have
small pockets that catch words from a walker's
lips, light from the moon's bright lyre.

6
No one thing immediately changes into another. A
million steps are taken before you reach the place
where one more step takes you across the border.

7
Edges change day by day by day. A wall falls
down. A gate opens. An ocean eats the coast
and a volcano spawns a new island.

Negotiations of form are endless.

8
We learn to be patient as stars. We sit in silence
for the coming and going of many suns. We speak
when we are moved and there is no need for
translation: instead a direct transfusion of

meaning passes between us.

Crow, lichen, thunder.

In this way we share truths we did not know
we knew but were set upon this orbiting planet
to discover.

9
I remember the land and the land remembers me.
Together we make memory. My heart lights up at
the sight of so many friends who greet me along
the way.

10
I am not the first stone to speak and I will not be
the last.

N.B. *First published in* Stone Talks, *2019, Triarchy Press*

Bare
by Dorinda Wegener

I have neglected my canning
for a full season spent in search
of a maid wreathed by wild

spicewood, alive and showy,
yet just: this hulled sunflower
where dark-eyed juncos mob

millet and cracked corn
among the March brush. A thaw
and depressions pock

nests of grasses, moss to couch
clutches of brown blotched eggs; soon
winter bird, two weeks less a day

young will leave upon fledging
while the last frost falls across field
and the farm cat hastens its hunt–

I have no words for lack that holds
late into a mother's spring
harder than the blue ice.

MENOPAUSE MIGRATION

by Caitlín Matthews

They pass, the bright dancers, down the long path of blood,

Leaving an empty story and a kicked-off shoe on the sod.

There's only a drift of music through the daily market's cry

And a long regret that impeaches the innocent Lenten sky.

Each of the dancing partners who swung me in their sway

Have passed like smoke from a hearthfire on a burning summer's day.

The passionate feet that bore me now dance to a different tune,

The love that was bright between us, turns dark as the changing moon.

I search for the shards of story upon a jagged shore,

As Isis in her mourning sought for the scattered lore.

Only the plaintive curlew its solitary fluting makes,

As over the barren hillside an empty morning breaks.

The hollow daylight departing, I lift my pleading eyes,

And out of the gentle darkness, see destiny's star arise.

Down its shimmering pathway, the ancient promises ride,

A hope that the dancing had blinded, a sure and certain guide.

A melody pure and perfect, a song from the heart of time,

Reverberates the darkness, making the dead boughs chime.

Fruits set on the fruitless branches as stars come tumbling out,

An untold story dances on the shivering shores of doubt.

a house to come back to against all odds
poem by Mireille Gansel; translation by Joan Seliger Sidney

to leave from a small fishing port or from some pier at the bottom of a
cove at the tides and currents to dock on makeshift pontoons water from
the only well on the island light from flashlights or candles all around you
murmurs and whispers voices and calls the slapping of beaks and the
rubbing of wings of these great travelers come from every continent on
the rocks and cliffs beaten by the winds day and night without a sound
with silent steps you become a bird among the birds and they become
inhabitants of the earth the time just the time to give life and to prepare
their young for the coming migration-

an outcrop of peat and rocks
poem by Mireille Gansel; translation by Joan Seliger Sidney

an outcrop of peat and rocks a whole underground world galleries and
burrows of seabirds arid land where they return from continents and
oceans to find their little homes buried deep under the wind-blown grass
an entire world of survival that you ignore when you step on it leaving
the narrow marked path fragile land their native land where they give life-

puffins
poem by Mireille Gansel; translation by Joan Seliger Sidney

I

returned from so far away their time becomes yours they are walking
a stone's throw from you so strange so familiar they come out of their
burrow with a little bit of dirt around their beak they wander around
watch scrutinize suddenly run to gather momentum to dive towards the
sea to the very bottom to disappear deep in the water to resurface with
a beak full of fish to dash off underground towards the little one at the
very bottom-

II

sudden wind of panic the great wings of the gulls cast their shadow on
the burrows the puffins sink into the earth stand guard run in tight rows
toward the promontory fly away without a cry-

III

standing at the edge of the cliff in the face of raging winds they are their
own little home-

IV

on the grassy slope they are there standing at the entrance of their
burrows like so many small transhumant huts on an alpine pasture in this
evening light-

Farne Islands early August
poem by Mireille Gansel; translation by Joan Seliger Sidney

in the small port of Seahouses upon raising anchor this morning the
fishermen said firmly: "They are gone. Yesterday, there were only two
Arctic terns left"-

at the edge of the rainy sky there are bright cumulus clouds with
translucent blue crater lakes the boat runs alongside the cliffs and their
silence already of absence and in a farewell dance all around the lantern
where in foggy weather we lit alarm fires two pair of wings so white so
thin barely the weight of a large letter they twirl before flight further
north where they fortify themselves until Antarctica where they will
arrive in November and on the desert island the bird burrows are empty
the expanses of pale green hemlock and pearl gray thistles tremble in
the wind and among the already black grass a puffin all alone among the
miniscule forget-me-nots and the silvery reflections of the last maritime
silenes a few little ones practice on the waves the leaden sky is so low that
the water has colors of night but suddenly a sunny spell traces a silver
bridge and then on the damp peat there is the scent of tall mint recently
pulled up for when the Arctic terns will come back to make their nests-

like a message to N.D.
who works on the island with the observatory
of Wildlife of the Country of Wales
poem by Mireille Gansel; translation by Joan Seliger Sidney

I

that night you recorded the forty-minute dialogue between the male and
female couple of English puffins at the bottom of their burrow-

II

before music, for me, there were sounds,
before sound became music sound was a
vector, sound, noise, melody, timbre,
was a vector almost louder than words
Sonia Wieder-Atherton

you dream of one day being able to recognize among a thousand each
one of these migratory birds when it will return next season among a
thousand to recognize its sounds its noises its movements its cries. Its
language-

and instead of a band know by his voice the storm petrel-

N.B. *These poems are forthcoming in* Soul House *by Mireille Gansel, translated by
Joan Seliger Sidney (New York: World Poetry, 2023)*

The Night Seals of Lubec
by Rodger Martin

At witching hour, summer rain patters on the wharf;
fog drifts in and out to a tide just before change.
The seals glide to the landing, ease themselves from the water.
Respectful of whiskers, they nuzzle with their brothers,
the sleeping dogs of Lubec, reminding them of kinship.
Then, through the open windows of the town,
the seals silently enter the bedrooms of sleepers.
The dogs of Lubec curl contentedly on the floor
while the seals whisper in the ears of dreamers
who've mastered the seas at midnight
and charted the oceans of the past.
Then, silky as they had arrived, the seals
leave the sleepers for dawn, gather again
at the edge of harbor, nuzzle again with their brothers
and depart. When the children wake, they speak
of graceful dives through sun-greened kelp.
Their elders wake to puzzlement at a thin film of water
on the tiles that lead to open windows.

N.B. *this poem originally appeared in* Crosswinds, *2019*

Choreography
by Patrice Pinette

~After Barry Lopez, "Winter Herons"

The story bothered me; it was beautiful,
but didn't go anywhere other
than Colorado and New York.
There was a lover loving, as if
from a distance. He admired
her on and off the stage—a dancer.
The heart—where was it?
Landing on the island
between uptown and downtown
traffic in the middle of Manhattan
on a snowy evening: great blue herons.
Settling a while under the pale light
of street lamps. White field
in the middle of the man
waiting, watching them wait
before shaking off their wings
and rising to an inaudible chord—
the whole troupe stroking the storm
as one heading north.

Magnetic Storm
by Patrice Pinette

Over snow beyond moonlight
solar flares
make the sky pulse

watching from a night field
in wind my pulse keeps time
or fear

bare trees bend in the tide
that shakes me too
attached to which branch

my family had no prayers
I made my own
years gust and pass

I want to say pray with me
I have not seen heaven
signal like this

~

On the snowmobile trail
    we sink up to our knees laughing
the gale makes us feel small

I hold onto my friends not to be blown over
    not to lose ground on this
New Hampshire hilltop that has been home

before leaving I will read the space around you
    and there it flares! I learn to scan
the whole sky even the moon alert

to what the long arm of the sun stirs up
    our little powers flicker

~

Animals pass through the wind
waiting to reappear
we think they are gone

but what do we know
of how spirit moves over the land
at a time like this preparing spring

sensing what can't be seen
we tremble
and turn back to the house

~

To stay
grounded
I kneel

a stunted pine
high up clinging
to stone
not to break

my shadow
punctuates moonlight
on blue snow

~

Later we drink tea from lemon balm passion
flower and mugwort to help us remember
our snow dreams out of the wind

we talk about leaving Abbot Hill soon
and how after our young student died suddenly
we could still feel her close to this land and sky

the eagle appeared three times
twice in the cards
then flying where no one expected

like one of the names for grief
charging the field
as what electric love we have flares forth

Canada Goose (The Canada Goose mates for life)
by Tina Meyer

1.

Our plan is to head south when you are well again
and rejoin the flock.
We are afraid now that the V has disappeared,
but we've found a field for food,
a nearby pond for water and warm marsh grass to rest in.

2.

Time has passed.

The daylight has grown shorter, the air more chilled.
I feed you as much as you can take, but you are weak.
I share my water, spitting it into you.
I have kept your feathers clean.
I sleep as close to you as I can so that you know I am here.
I often think of the flock.

3.

More time has passed.

Today, you could not get up.
I brought you some dried grass,
but the pond surface has frozen.
I must wait for water.
I fear the fox.
I smell it; I will stay vigilant.
Don't worry, I am near.
I will keep your graceful head under my wing so that you know
you're not alone.
I will not leave you.

4.

It is dawn.
For some time now, your breathing has stilled.
I have been awake all night,
watching for the fox.
I have spent many hours admiring your beautiful stripes.

It is hard for me to leave you behind,
especially for the fox.
I will wait until mid-day when it is asleep.

Then,
forever alone now,

I will try and find south.

Brought Me to My Knees
by Claire Millikin

Heat my skin remembers from childhood in Georgia pulls
as if I were tugged through a door, past some desiccated front porch
where shelves of seeds and sticks store a thick scent
of salt-sharpened earth.

No one else here, too hot today.
But I have a calendar to keep, and tidal seasons never sleep.
Cordgrass toughening like girls asked the wrong questions too early,
eelgrass sinking in tall-limbed water.

The sky fits bowl-tight to horizon's flat glass.
Nouns are only mirrors lifting in blue stiffness.
Without breeze the marsh feels abandoned,
footlands of this rising century,

and it brings me to my knees to feel the water so swelling,
throwing salt deeper inland against unprotected roots.
In the still silence of hard heat, I hear exhausted animals
and think of my parents' house,

how after they'd fight, not argue, fight,
the quiet girls we'd become then, hiding in Lou's closet.
A salt marsh, you see, is made of cuts
like that place in love where you resurrect what's left.

Little bruises, the delicate whorls in grasses,
last night's fitful dream's imprint.
Star-nosed moles touch their way
through this world from which we cannot entirely awaken.

A haiku
by Tammi J Truax

wildflowers teem
acres of unfettered land
only one monarch

Daucus Carota
by Tammi J Truax

At Pleasant Hill Preserve
under the Emerson Elm
the Queen Anne's Lace
performs a dainty dance
to the muted music
of a slow summer breeze.

The flower's name, a fairy tale;
Queen Anne, a fine tatter,
one day pricked herself,
and a drop of her blood
plopped upon her lace,
leaving a purpled floret
in the center of a flower.

Fiction at its finest,
for Queen Anne's Lace
is actually a commoner.
A workhorse called *Wild Carrot.*
She's a host plant for the
black swallowtail butterfly
and a variety of aphids.

Her prodigious seeds feed
the ring-necked pheasant and pine mouse.
Roaming rabbits and white-tailed deer
stop by to enjoy a few nibbles
of her fresh flower and fern.
Her fluffy foliage provides the preferred
building material for nesting starlings.

And now, in my America,
I suspect, I fear
our sisters, our daughters
will harvest the maiden's lace,

as women have done in
the uncivilized before-times,
from India to Appalachia,
as an abortifacient.

Taken the morning after,
the Queen's seeds chewed
or crushed into a tea or slurry,
swallowed with greater doses
of desperation and prayer.

The real life maidens wait
for the purplish droplet to come,
for her womb to imitate the flower,
for whom, without patriarchal control,
as the seeds ripen, the blossom
curls inward to form a tight nest shape,
turns a brownish color, in an act

of self-preservation,
of self-protection,
of survival.

Cassidy's Pub
by Elaine Reardon

It meant nothing more than a pint
in the pub. We chatted over pints,
briefcases and handbags stowed,
sweaters and raincoats tossed over
chairs. Francis said Michael Collins

frequented Cassidy's Pub. Collins arrived
from Cork and put his own life
into the wind. Now on O'Connell Street
people rest on benches and contemplate
in The Garden of Remembrance, created

for children of *Ireland in the coming times*,
inheritance for coming *generations of hope*.
Our mythology, children changed to swans,
the new peace manifest into form, Word made
Sacred, life sacred. Transformation into peace.

In these days of soft border crossings, people
speak of the country to the north. In our time
of healing, Brexit has come like a fox among
rabbits. On both sides of the border we ask
Will the Good Friday Peace Agreement hold?

Written at the Tavern
by Sean Prentiss

Four years mortgaged to the city
mortgaged to a career job
how many more moons until
I am brave enough for home

Into the City
by Sean Prentiss

Now that I've come here, into the city,
deep into tall towers that don't lean
into an embrace like mountains do
—rather blot out our sun—I wonder

why.

Autumn of the Heart
by Sean Prentiss

Autumn hearts cannot sleep with all
the geese singing of home as they fly

above the cold bones of this house.
Their calls empty as wind and gone

as quickly toward whatever next home.
But with this house fused to concrete

and blacktop that pools water, soon
our geese, not knowing better, might

mistake this gathered water for their
next stop. I too am rooted in the wrong

ways and left bleating for home.

Testament
by Patrick Curry

I have no heavenly home.
The only place I know is here,
in the ruck and roil of gathering waters
recoiling upon themselves,
the air congealing into a troubling warmth,
the inconstant light, kindling and dying,
and the Earth, birthing-bed and bier,
moving beneath us

But at the end of the path
along the abandoned reservoir,
I plant my stick on a corner
of the rotting cement block
and for a moment, everything –

The gaze of the unbearably
bright sun-god through the leaves,
shaken by a gust of emotion;
the imbecilic roar from the road
and overhead, as the dull dragons coast
into Heathrow; and the great old plane-tree,
vulnerable as truth, somehow escaped
from the wreck –

Everything coalesces
into a whole, perfect in itself,
that in another moment
is no more

Winnipeg
by Patrick Curry

I.m. Robinson Jeffers

All this detritus left behind
when capital last roared through –
downtown a corporate wasteland, giving way
to strip malls, jumped-up jeeps, drug marts
and cheap fast food –
the prairie, crouched, is waiting
to reclaim:

The tawny scrub, African
in its dry soul
The spindly trees, shaved off at mid-height
by a giant hand of cold
The dishevelled ice, in stately sail
down the sullen brown river
And the crows, mob-handed,
shouting

Not long now
not long now

N.B. *This poem has previously appeared in the online journal* The Ecological Citizen

Winter Intake
by Jesse LoVasco

Following footpaths through the woods
in winter, I take steps on crusty ice,
as naked trees crackle, while sap runs slow.

I breathe frigid air, booting about pines
and hemlock, see seeds hooded in snowcaps,
boulders and hills, and a frozen waterfall stair.

This white landscape is written on, like paper,
in the language of tracks.
Deer and fox prints write sentences
of their story on snow;

patterns of a chase,
a scampering squirrel,
wing print stretched across a snowbank,
where hawk hunted prey.

I lie down in the center
of a grove of Birch trees
facing the ice blue sky,
my warm skin merging with cold,
fusing into a frozen snow-bed.

Crystal laced wind, sparkles down
from the canopy. I open my mouth
to taste hundreds of frosted stars.

As Hemlocks of the Forest
by Jesse LoVasco

we have existed thousands of years,
elders in a deep green ecosystem,
standing brave, while threatening waves
of death move among us.

As something so small can kill us.

We live three to eight hundred years
as witnesses of birth and death,
bird, fox, coyote and deer, passing
seasons, swelling storms.

As something so small can kill us.

Our brethren, Birch, Maple and Oak,
will spread over our ghost shadows,
replace spaces we grew in, reaching
their roots and changing the canopy.

As something so small can kill us.

From our dead trunks grow Reishi,
the parasitic fungi, shiny red, orange,
and white-rimmed mushrooms,
that serve as medicine.

As something so small can kill us.

If you walk through the forest and see
us, reach out and hold the flat, underside
needles of our hands in yours, that we will
endure inevitable times of extinction.

As the Wooly Adelgid, so small, can kill us.

Death Brings Life to a Forest
by Jesse LoVasco

Mud colored   skeletons   of Joe Pye Weed
                    and Golden Rod

hold up soft puffs of seed, like wands, ready to take off with the wind.

Tawny
            brown, gold and
                            orange leaves
                                        lie scattered on the ground.

Golden mushrooms   protrude from   a hole in Hemlock.

Sumac leaves   voice their   departure in bright red.

Death brings light to a forest.

            as beams of sun pass between fallen trees.

Hidden things begin to appear,

                        witch's brooms, nests, mushrooms,

            small altars of sticks, leaves and stones.

A decomposing graveyard of tree trunks

                grow a mass of moss,   swallowing them into the
forest floor.

One golden beech tree,   waving sunlight on leaves like a beacon,

brown marcessant leaves,   clinging

like a child attached to the skirts of a mother.

Green ferns turn to white lace.

Seven black crows and a screeching squirrel

                    move across the canopy claiming their territory,

and I leave a witness,   to how death reveals it's story in a season,

takes life back and makes it into something new.

To Be Under Your Spell
by Jesse LoVasco

I am taking hesitant steps,
entering this cathedral
of trees, guilds of fern,
moss and lichen, knowing
I will not want to leave.

Afraid that once I know you,
my body will thirst,
hunger for your moisture,
veins filling like sap,

wanting to linger among
your roots and boulders.
Just like lovers
who kiss between sheets
at sunrise, linger.

Then departing through a door,
I may weaken without your scent,
the sound of wind whirring
through evergreen and
deciduous leaves.

Witch's Broom
by Jesse LoVasco

I was once
haunted by a
witch, riding
across the moon
on her broom,

fang toothed and
pointed chin,
following me
from the sky.
I could not
escape her
piercing eyes.

A silhouette
of her disguise hangs
in a snarl of branches,
tangled like hair,
clumped on a tree
found after leaves
release in the air.

Whorled and woody,
collecting wind debris
a fungi spreading
wildly, hidden,
not seen.

A ghostly shadow,
a stranger in a
stand, a presence
of darkness
on the trails
of this forest land.

Flying at Night
by Janet MacFadyen

Somewhere in the North Atlantic
fishermen winnow the sea until nothing is left
except sadness. The fields
never lay fallow, scraped to the bones
of shimmering fish.

A curtain of snow
sweeps across waves so thick
you couldn't see your nose, if you were there and not
three miles high, blind, ear-budded,
breathing by umbilicus
to the carbon fiber webbing.

Out of mind, flocks of seabirds float,
scattered plashes of white, and polar bears
hitch rides on waxy slicks from Greenland
to Baffin Island.

The sea could be pewter,
a length of silk stretched over
our waiting bones. The sleeper
gathers a dark shawl of bubbles
around her shoulders, the edge of surf
under her chin. The dream becomes

thirst in an ocean of salt,
what we have always desired, held dear
to our hearts. I could write all night about
this not knowing—trying to knit together
what our hearts divulge and our dreams ensnare,
while far below whales sleep with one eye open
and the other eye closed.

What It Takes
by Janet MacFadyen

I was being buzzed again by messengers
who tell me to wake up from nightmares. This time
I was in a circle of friends, all of us ill
from some heaviness that seeped
through our blood like anesthesia.
It was hard to feel and in any case

I had lost the habit years ago. The pen
that wrote the words shriveled to a thread
leaving a vague anxiety as I dressed
and readied myself for something,
I don't remember what.

Later stomach cancer ushered out
my oldest friend. The news came sandwiched
between shootings — El Paso and Dayton —and I asked
how much more could I digest

before I too sickened and died. Then I killed
the mosquito who lit on my wrist to bleed me, the wrist
that always aches with numbness. But nature
is profligate: soon another messenger

explored my lips and my breath.
We are just landscapes to these beings that whir
about our ears trying to make us face

what lies ahead. When the glass
of my memory is trained on the future it finds
a continuing darkness, both the deep soil where bulbs

tighten to green arrows of intention
and a chaotic field of war. My family's people
believed in paving their way relentlessly forward

and it looks like we have paved ourselves over.
The traffic roars above, away from somewhere

toward somewhere else, drowning out
any instruction. None of us have been taught

how to prepare for this next voyage.

Bitterroot
by DJ Lee

I walk the land in early spring, coat pulled tight against the wind. Bunchgrass winces underfoot. Death camas leans against basalt, golden current parades her bright blooms. I'm looking for bitterroot among tufts of buckwheat.

Once, at York Minster, the largest Medieval cathedral in England, I stood awestruck by twenty-five massive glass mosaics depicting Biblical scenes. Christ in scraggy beard and high forehead holding up two fingers in the sign of the cross. Something about the light on glass made me think of transcendence. His head capped by a flowered cloth.

Bitterroots have pink flowers and long, thin roots. A staple for those who travelled the mountains and valleys of this place. The plant that came when people needed it most, midwinter spring, their migrations coinciding with the bitterroot's movement from the underworld to this one.

A salvation story: an ounce of dried root provides enough nourishment for a meal.

A Salish story: a long time ago, a drought scorched this land and sucked the plants dry. Animals withered; people starved. A grandmother left the famished village and sang a death song, spilling tears into her gray, stringy hair. As she wept, a bird descended and turned her tears to blood-colored flowers with bitter roots like her own hair.

When Lewis and Clark passed south of here, they, too, were starving. Lewis is said to have *discovered* the bitterroot. The plant bears his name, *Lewisia rediviva.*

Before white settlement, the Spokane, Nimiipuu, Salish, and Kalispell people gathered for a ritual that began with a prayer spoken by an old woman in honor of the starving grandmother. The community harvested the starchy root and feasted.

In 1805, Lewis wrote: "They become perfectly soft by boiling, but had a very bitter taste, which was nauseous to my palate, and I transferred them to the Indians who had eat them heartily." Bitterroot gave him diarrhea. A botanist chose the genus name *Lewisia* perhaps joking about Lewis' digestive problems. The specific epithet, *redivivus*, comes from Medieval Latin rɛdɪˈvaɪvəs—resurrection. The botanists in Philadelphia charged with organizing Lewis' plants collection noticed a green flicker of life in the dead bitterroot. When they planted it, it flowered.

In York Minster cathedral, the lower panel of Christ's resurrection shows two soldiers guarding the grave. They don't see the risen Christ. Sitting in dejection, they're encased in gray-white glass like the milky roots of a plant. Christ's eyes bulge. The left one droops toward Earth. When I saw the eye illuminated, I felt the sense of sprouting.

Bitter roots. My grandmother once lived near this land at the Jane O'Brien Sanitarium. I remember in her garden, how alongside lettuce, melon, raspberries, beans, carrots, potatoes, and zucchini, she grew bitterroots. Zucchinis have shallow roots killed by frost. Every year, in the slant light of autumn, she uprooted hundreds of zucchinis while their leaves were still green. She brought them inside bunched together, a family of greens. Later, she minced them into the compost at the back of the garden. Spring, she used that soil to feed the next generation of plants.

I walk the land in early spring, coat pulled tight against the clouds. Pass a large boulder with RIP spray painted on its flank. A cairn with a handwritten tribute to a mother buried inside. The bitterroots are still asleep.

When I think of the bitterroot, I try to balance the grandmother crying for her starving children with starving Lewis exploring and exploiting the West.

Bitterroots are deep-routed, stories woven through families and cultures.

Mima Mound
by DJ Lee

after Keith Leonard

Though the mima mound is piled earth
it is not a grave, but like a grave
holds our bones, the mima mound entombs
silt, sand, pebbles, pocket gophers,
long-toed salamanders, and each kidney-shaped salamander
lives unseen beneath rotted logs and loose bark,
in cool damp depressions,
creeping out by night,
illumined by the silent moon,
and I couldn't know
the stab in my kidney was a lump
interred in my abdomen,
a mound swelling in the midnight of my body,
until it was lit up by the ultrasound
and cut out by the wire loop
in the fevered room,
and though I was shrouded in gowns,
the room didn't smell of death,
but like the smell of death,
it was an urgent reminder to live
close to the piled earth,
to the feathery canary grass,
to the flame-resistant ponderosas,
where salamanders born of fire,
golden stripes down their backs,
thrive under the bulging mima mound.

Yarra Yarra
by Earl Livings (*Further than Night*, Bystander Press, Melbourne, 2000)

You are what land has made you
As you define land.
You are urgency of rain,
Stubborn compliance of soil and rock,
Fountain and erosion of mountains.
You are winnowing of light through leaf and bark,
Flash of eel and diving waterfowl,
Sweep and tumble of river-stone.
You are branch-tips dipping into you
With wind that commands you from air.
You are swift memory of sky
And haunt of dragonflies.
You are keen edge of air and water,
Water and earth, earth and shadow.
Your constant beginning is foretold
During lessons that render time
In firelight and breath of song,
In scored paintings on bark,
In patterns of dust dancing feet raise.
From drag marks of a shuffling old man
To freedom of water-locked land
Carved open by heroes with stone axes,
You are everything in everything.

And always seasons urge your people
To their seasoned ways.
Your banks know chatter of digging women,
Know silent stance of hunters.
Your trees throw shade over cooking fires
And the gathering circles.
Your water is sustenance,
Is play of bodies and froth.
There is no end to you as your people
Honour the bounty of your flow
In trace of seasons

From mountain to sea.
There is no end to you
Even when your people are at an end.

Another time, another people,
And they, for a moment,
Tilt their heads to shifting shadows
Artificial lights cannot dismiss,
Then resume their habits.
For them, your banks and river-beds
Are clay for brick-kilns.
For them, your flow is challenge
For punt and bridge, a terse crossing
For those who come to tame your trees.
For them, the growing land beyond
Is fodder for simple impulse of pursuit.
You are echoes of bonfires fading
Into sobriety of church socials.
You are seasonal excuse for pipelines
And multiplicity of roads.
You are demarcation of our plots.

And we are drawn to you.
You are silt of our past,
Sludge of our chemistry,
Gleam of our ships and tankers.
Under umbrellas, at picnic tables,
Feeding stale bread to ducks,
Tossing sticks for ardent dogs,
Walking mirror-strides with lovers,
Rowing upstream with careful children,
Gasping as we pause along a concrete track,
Stopping in rigid traffic on your bridges,
We are keen to swing above you,
Mouth poised between laughter and fear
The moment hands are free
Of the horizontal rope,
And you rush to greet us,
Without end.

Foxglove, or 'snoxum'
by Katherine Pierpoint

foxglove, snoxum, gloves of the Virgin,
finger-hat, dog's lug,
whitethroat, plantain —
this smatter-path of freckles,
these leopard-print dance-steps
stippled in purple;
all draw the solemnly drunken bees.

Bees tumble   so precisely
          in and out
of the different worlds of flowers —
short-focussed, fat angels at work,
          intent
on the dotted paths,
the goldenrod, the rose.

Hummingwinged,
they swing down into the foxglove's bell,
and these bees furrow, they
          wade, half-blind, up deep channels of perfume
to the bright, domed chambers inside each heart.

Black ankle-joints all dusted in gold,
          tiny gauntleted wrists;
but now each bee's a barge — dark, bull-nosed and laden,
pulled home by the sun.

Up   and down
all their lives
in the light.

Foxglove, crab-apple, astrantia, vine.

Still circling, nearly-finishing, never resting
say the bees

I'll see you on the other side of the rose
says each rose.

N.B. shortlisted for the Bridport prize, 2017

The Twist in the River
by Katherine Pierpoint

At the clear, beer-coloured and bubbleshot twist in the river—
Every stone a speckled egg spawned in that deep lap,
Every pockmarked, pitted pebble a planet, blindly seeing through its own
evolution -
The shallows, and the tall air, are filled with sound and light.
This part of the river expects to be seen, for it has drawn you there,
And the trees, selfless, introduce the sky into your love for the water.
If this place were a person, it would be making up a paper hat while
humming,
Entirely self-contained, absorbed yet radiant—
A family moment, appearing normal until years later in retrospect,
When its depths are fully felt, beyond blunt experience.

Underwater, the light thickens slightly but never sets
And the river runs through its own fingers, careless.

N.B. *from* Truffle Beds *(Faber, 1995), p.1*

Moonapple
by Katherine Pierpoint

Long, silver linenfolds of grass
slip, coolly, round the apple-tree.

The moon, as the mirror, cannot ripen.
It can fill, can spill -
can see, but not embrace, the tree.

This light shower of iron filings
has fallen   far from the quickening magnet,
forgotten how to dance.

Now the wind streams downmoon
and the apple-leaves flip, slim as fish in a net.

The moon is the bland face of an upswung hammer;
it beats each silver leaf
to the wooden frame.

One early apple, still half a flower closing,
and half stem-filling
lets go -
a meteor
into the running surf of grass

to be cratered by insects
who dig in bliss, and blind meander;
diving mouth-first, in spirals
towards the core.

N.B. privately published by the Hawthorn Press, 2000

Bee Longing
by Cathryn Hankla

Crawling the battlefield,
     trapped borer bee grips

brothers, sisters, implores
      eyes to eyes, shining

dark bent fractals. I can't
     pretend to love much

about these plump slow
      bees trailing saw dust

to mark fraught tunneling.
     This carpenter bee,

entranced and entrapped, crawled
      in eco-seeking

to lay its eggs, instead
    it will join these dead.

But this is my home— this
     boundary means we

live here now, yet brother
     buzz must be with us.

View from a Hillside Overlooking Lake Champlain
by Dan Close

Stand on this hill
and, facing west, then
— stretch out your arms to north and south —

then gaze below them at the length of lake
and look to right and left
and see Champlain stretch well beyond the reaches of your fingertips
until it curls and bends and disappears into the distance.
In olden times, it had a different name.
They called it, then, The Sea Between.

Look now across the lake at Adirondack ranges in the west —
six or seven ranges you can see from here at least
stretch far and further into the dimness of the mist,
and if you look with care, and if you have the gift,
you can see the old gods on the highest ridges of those ranges
brandishing their war clubs and their lances —

But let that vision go.
Look down upon this land that leads down to the lake.
There is a softer, simpler beauty in this land;
a quiet beauty worked into the land like lace.
Below us are the hayfields, some left fallow
for the bobolinks and larks to sing
and skylark in.

Before your eyes stand rows of oaks indifferent in their majesty,
then great swaths of forest green — maple, cedar, ash, and
shagbark hickory,
and lower still, bogs quiet in the day
except for froggies tuning up for evening songfests and display,
and scattered all about small houses for the bluebirds
that you see as flashing points of almost neon light.

And all of this grand panorama has been saved
for you and countless other animals and birds

and flowers of the fields and forests and of
mountain bogs and vernal pools.
Go now and take the trail, and ramble round this
saving grace of nature,
this refuge saved for all the future time
that we can see,
this parcel subtle as the earth is long.
All elements rejoice, and raise their souls in song.
Drink in this beauty, bright and deep.
Forever, it is yours to keep.

DUCK! Here Comes the Train!
by Dan Close

At midday when the train from Rutland comes
        a-flying up the new-laid track
It hums, and hums, and hums, and hoots, and shrugs
        and comes on strong
And you can hear it as it grinds along
        bringing the cement and oil
            to Burlington
Because the hum is in the track, besides the
        clickety-clack, clickety-clack
And the whole world moves along with that
        and resonates in ears and even in your feet.

Over the hills and far away; over the hills and gone –
        the right-of-way still sings its terrible infernal song.
A taking of the land is what it is.
        If only for a minute of the day
The power of the rail takes nature's soul away.

But I sit on a bench, hard by the track, that
        overlooks a tarn,
and in the quiet of the day I see a calm
deep here inside the darkest woods, after
        the freight train's gone.
After the diesel's shudder, after the diesel's moan
the chittering chipmunk comes calling
wondering if I bear a gift of crumbs.
Small warblers flit among the undergrowth
        wearing white bellies and gray overcoats
And towhees scratch among the fallen leaves
        for lunches of their own that Nature on its own provides.

And then I see a ripple on the water's edge
        and then a Wood Duck pops out of the sedge,
        propels himself across the pond, quiet as a mouse,
        then joined by, possibly, his spouse, and then

four more of them, the males with brightest
      colors round their heads, and all of them
           intent on quietude.
They do not spy me spying them from my woodland bench,
      and I, I watch their quiet paddling
         as they go by.
And all of us seem quite content to listen to
      the falling leaves of autumn
          hit the ground without a sound except
             for when they come down from the sky
          and hit the curled-up leaves of days gone by.

Critters of the Charlotte Refuge
by Dan Close

Monarchs of the Realm

The Monarchs fly in spring and fall;
In spring, they're hardly seen at all,
But in the fall, they flutter by
And look like oak leaves as they fly,
Or like a wing of areoplanes
They swoop down from their high domains
From thermal lifts of mighty length
And light on milkweed, gain their strength,
Then up into the sky they go
To get far south before the snow,
And powered by the goldenrod's sweet nectar
They'll not be seen again this year, if ever.
But they will still their destinations plot
And end up where it's nice and hot.

The Bobcat

The bobcat that runs down the lane
Takes off like a shot, might and main
Grabs a rabbit or two
Enough for a stew
And thus she completes the food chain.

Twilight of the Frogs
by Dan Close

The symphony of frogs starts up in the Spring
When the Chorus Frogs begin to sing,
And these are followed by the piercing violins
Of Peepers, yes, Spring Peepers, that sing the springtime in.
The Wood Frogs, woodwinds, gronk their monosyllables amain;
And Tree Frog piccolos are heard this springtime once again.
Staccato Leopard Frogs are all the rage
As their percussion section takes the stage;
While Green Frogs come upon the stage so late
They must tune up – their single strings vibrate.
American Toads, high up in the trees,
Sing such shrieking sopranos you'd hardly believe
Weren't some kind of jungle cat, or maybe baboon,
And Bullfrogs chime in with tubas and bassoons.
Harrumph! Harrumph! Harrumph di di aye yi yi yi yi
Harrumph! Harrumph! Harrumph di di aye aye yi yi yi
Harrumph! Harrumph! Harrumph di di aye yi yi yi yi
Harrumph! Harrumph! Harrumph di di aye aye yi yi yi

And on into the night this cacophony does ring:
Exuberating exhilarants exhilarating sing!
Let's hope this stays, this twilight of the frogs,
And doesn't portend the twilight of these woodland gods.

Resisting the Lilacs
by Kathy Kremins

It seems as if there
are lilacs everywhere
tempting me,
peeking just above
the bedroom windowsill
to see if I am looking
smelling the scent
released in pulses
by intermittent wind,
swatting the luscious smell
around like a cat with a yarn ball.
Even in my secret spot on the hill,
lilac bush pushes itself
into the edges of my vision,
peripheral fragrance
luring me to turn
to see the butterflies,
two of them, both yellow and black,
licking and tasting the purple curls,
hovering for a moment
in erotic pause
while I go wild,
resisting the lilacs
has become my hairshirt,
my penance for all I have displaced,
picked flowers, pulled weeds,
plucked roses, cut grass,
a test against temptations,
the fantasy of my body bathed in lilac,
committing sins.

The Swifts Return
by Roger Lebovitz

The swifts return each May after flying thousands of miles from another continent. I have never been quite sure where they winter or how they travel the long distances from their wintering ground to their summer homes. They nest inside chimneys, and on warm evenings you can hear how they are calling to one another high up in the middle of the air, and watch their little bodies flit up and down in great near-invisible motions. The brick chimneys in which they put their nests are made out of clay found on the floor of the old sea that vanished thousand years ago. This clay represents the smallest particle of the lands worn away by the rivers that carried their burdens to this old sea. So that each nest is built inside a tower risen, in fact, from the bottom of the ocean. The chimney bricks are fired in a process as old, perhaps, as the Tower of Babel. It is said that once the Tower had been destroyed, the remnant still standing hosted a colony of swift nests for many years afterwards. If you look carefully at Brueghel's painting of the Tower you might imagine a few spots in the sky that could be swifts, and the swift's call may well retain some of the sound of the universal language spoken before the Tower's destruction. But this is all speculation. Yet I firmly believe nothing can be truly desolate if there are swifts. When they return in the spring and I look up in the sky to see them, it seems as if they never left. As if there were no such thing as a vacant sky.

Toward the Lake
at the mouth of the Little North Fork
by Robert Wrigley

The river's purposeful, immemorial unwandering,
the curvaceous meander and bee-line of it
down to the basin of heavy metal tea.

Its dearth in autumn, its abundance in spring,
a live fallen cedar with root wad run aground
mid-channel in May? Holding water in October.

Burble, wash, sough, diminishing plunge
and thrash, its cold and never-still depths,
into stiller ones, to slow and swirl, to rest in the lake,

for the long massive migration that lies ahead,
from river to river to river to river,
to the planet it helps make of the sea.

River Pledge

on the North Fork of the Coeur d'Alene

by Robert Wrigley

Runs, riffles, rapids, and rills,
the river says goodbye hello, hello
goodbye, and all the bird songs
say the same exact thing only moreso.
The wildflowers' patriotic flags fly,
they pledge allegiance to the river
and the constitution of the sky,
history always the same and never
exactly, except for goodbye hello
hello goodbye forever.

Riverbed
by Robert Wrigley

Only the laces and scarves
of the waves remain
in what's left of the light,

which seems to lift but sinks,
soddening, washing away
in the cold mountain river.

Soon all that's seen is sound,
acoustics of the goings
shimmering into distance and night.

Then as the first star drifts
on the current's black tongue,
the tatting and embroidery

of froths is reborn as veils,
until the moon through timber
rolls its silver bolt of sheen

across the water, over
the river's abandonment to swirl
and passion where it lies.

As One Learns to Expect
by Robert Wrigley

The dragonfly hovers over the hole
where the river's current slackens into depth
and swoops down to take from the air
the tiny black flies known as trico,
or the white-winged curse, sometimes
come in hatches so thick the trout go mad
in feeding, so many bugs on the water
at once even your perfectly matched
imitation of feather and thread
is impossible to make out among them.

But this is a modest hatch, and as you make
your perfect cast, the tippet extended
in a slight curve, the fly sure to touch
the surface of the water first, the dragonfly
dives down to examine it as it falls
and follows it down to a foot above the surface,
from which bursts a shimmering cutthroat
almost as long as your arm, and it takes not
the fake you offered but the dragonfly,
and rises through a hundred further casts no more.

Along the River
  —North Fork of the Coeur d'Alene, Idaho
by Kim Barnes

The man I thought I loved
took me to the Snake Pit
for dinner on the table
and drinks behind the bar

then a dusky drive
upriver, through cottonwoods,
fir, and pine, across the floodplain
until the flat expanse rose

into palisades of basalt,
the channel narrowed,
the road fell to gravel,
the sky inked black

by the time we made
the hand-planked bridge
to Vera's, great aunt
who had raised him,

her homestead house
a warren of rooms
added on, added on,
the porch screened in,

an open-air bed,
where her only son
slept that night, the next day,
every night, every day, always,

a cedar stump beside him, bottle
and smokes, bottle and smokes
she paid for to keep him
not dead, not alive, but there

with her, the last of her family
except for the man
I thought I loved,
and lay with through the dark

hours in the single bed
upstairs, window open
to mosquitoes, spiders, flies--
intimacies of Mary's hard life,

I thought, good life, she said,
and took me to her garden
alongside the river, each
with a soup can of kerosene,

and we picked hornworms
from the tomatoes, beetles
from the squash, drowned
them in fuel, and she told me

of the day her new cookstove
arrived, rafted upstream, mules
either side, beautiful, she said,
a gift from her husband,

but more trustworthy and lasting,
like the river, she said,
and we went to the barn
to feed the fawn whose mother

she had shot and butchered, tidbits
preserved in Mason jars,
trout and grouse, too, still holding
their bones, cooked for our meals

on her beautiful stove
with roots from the cellar,
and I watched her fill a plate,
take it to her son, touch his silver

crown, knowing he would die
there of nothing more or less
than need for liquor and smoke,
or maybe from fire, may it take them

both, she said, and looked
at the man I thought I loved
then rested her eyes on me
but didn't speak until later,
while we washed and dried
side-by-side, the men, her kin,
on the porch, passing the bottle,
and she slid the ring from her finger,

slipped it onto mine, said,
marry the river, not the man,
and I was betrothed by her hand,
the water we looked across deeply

running, trout still, soundless
owl in the cedar grove,
rocks turning over as I slept,
a bride in her beautiful bed.

Rhubarb
       —*Ona's House, Wallace, Idaho*
by Kim Barnes

I want to plant rhubarb
in patches, in plats,
in old pots and dishpans,
a red-striped acre,
a sour mile of stalks
that will not last
but time enough
to lace with lemon,
pack with sugar,
preserve or bake, a bite
of spring in the mouth
when February is a shroud,
the night as long
as a day in the mine,
the moon skating
the iced river,
and I ask of the air
a little more warmth,
a little more light,
ice cream made of snow,
compote of hot rhubarb,
bright sun of my life.

Sonnet for a Fisherman
        by Angela Leighton

Now he's turned his back on the sea's
        livings, killings,
Pasquale docks a fleet of miniatures
        high-and-dry —
each plywood strip cambered, sealed,
        glossed ship-shape
to take the mountain ranges of the waves
        heaved in its way,
or any stormy dream that sweeps
        his sleeping brain.

Long days, he sits in an airless room
        to flitch and chip
the wood's life-saving way of being
        hollowed, prowed —
though each float sits on a cross of sticks
        unmoved, mid-air.

Now he's done with fishing, Pasquale
        nets no catch
except what a trawl of memory throws up:
        (don't look, don't touch,
the roll will take it out, disperse
        its pieces of a life.)
So he chisels another – will it ferry the load
        of souls who'd go
safe as houses for a home this night?
        But his craft's too light.
It keeps the finish of an art that know
        no human cargo.

N.B. *This poem is previously published in* Something, I forget *(Carcanet, 2023)*

The Last Word
by Carolyn Oulton

Inspired by:

'Lines on a scene nightly exhibited at Bousfield's Library, Margate'. Anon.
Kentish Gazette 21 August 1810.

"To the author of 'Lines on a scene nightly exhibited at Bousfield's Library, Margate'." A. H.
Kentish Gazette 24 August 1810.

Over the bay a ship,
clouds thickening. Salt
the shape of wings
blurs the window.
Sea a heap of shavings.
Birds jerk up
like bones holding a dress
against the body,
tear the sky
like silk
in a woman's fingers.

Soft venerable madam.
Night after night
her *ancient eyes*
sink into a young man's flesh.
Better for Eve to *stay*
at home with Adam.
Her feather inks his face –
had she not strayed from Adam,
come to that, *I ne'er had heard*
from you. And so
Most witty fool – adieu!

Both poems have been copied
in a female hand, perhaps
for inclusion in an album.
There is time
both to add this to my notebook
and to stare through glass,
where a ferry rips the seams
out of a silky sky.
I found them in Margate library.
The woman leaves by ship.
I invented the ending myself.

Not One But Many
by Kathryn Millar

I do not have one
I have many

I do not have one rock against the storms of life
But I have an awesome collection of stones scattered across life's ocean
that provides me
safe travel wherever I wish to go.

I do not have one that has been witness to my life
But I have many that hold the sacred pieces of my past
Times shared. Tears shed in loss and hope. Laughter infused memories.
Encouraging words and listening ears.

I do not have one to say good night to every night
But I have many who greet me at the door with the recognition of my
past, belief in my person and prayers for my possibility
Each one opening their hearts and homes to me as I pass through
Reminding me that I have a place
At any time
I am not alone
Always welcome

I do not have the one heart crushing, inevitable goodbye
But many heartfelt goodbyes that always come too soon.

Sometimes in the moments between
It is easy to feel alone
And easy to forget my long reaching roots
But I do not forget

I do not have one to hold me late into the night
But I have many holding me between the empty spaces creating rock
bridges so strong
I can not drown
I swing from these wide spread roots doing cartwheels in the sky

I do not have one
But I do have many

A Tumbledown of Rocks
by Kathryn Millar

Pebbles to stones to rocks
Create the trail, disguise the trail, give scope to the trail
Boulders as tall as I am
Taller than I am
Determine the path, guard the path, and confuse the path as I travel

And just when I think there could be no more rocks
I come to a garden of giant rocks
It rises straight up from where I stand
Puzzling my sense of direction
I search for blue blazes and wonder where the path could be
All I see are boulders and rocks, roots and my boots
Trees by my side and a sky hidden behind
Step-less until I spy it
The only discernible direction in this sea of rock bound chaos
A blue flash on an old tree trunk
Directing me to head further into this stone built journey
I wonder how I will conquer it
Or if I should even dare
I am as far from hiking as I am close to bouldering

Alone

When I turn around to look, I cannot see from where I started
I cannot see a trail or a path or a remnant of my travels

Rocks and courage are all that I have

Mushroom Circus
by Kathryn Millar

Light shimmers through the leaves a wide, big top crown
Sunlight speckles, shape-shifting on the ground
The scene a parade announcing the clowns

The mushrooms like clowns with wide speckled caps
Orange, brown, and blue inspiring formats
Trumpets, Chanterelles and Oysters do dance

Sprinkled across logs or rising from the soil
Vegetative growth Mycelium in the spoil
Toadstools appear at my feet from thin air

Filling the circus tent with wide ruffled collars
Climbing over branches like tumbling from cars
Each its own character on a mission to serve

My eyes search the landscape for clowns on a stroll
My eyes search the hippodrome that is the forest floor
Slightly exaggerated or wildly fantastic

These mushroom clowns are amusing
And I the recipient of their comical doings

Spring Beech
by Kathryn Millar

Hidden in the wooded frame
Of a wet spring landscape
Against stone grey skies
                                 and sleeping forest floors
Between the monochrome shapes of Maples and Oaks
Glowing in the Western Maine Woods

I discover the first flower of Spring

And it is not
                The Crocus
                        Bleeding Heart
                                or White Trillium

It is the Beech
                                Leaf

After six, long, Winter months
Still clinging to the branches
Almost incandescence these are
As they dangle
Slightly askew along Wind's consistent path

Ghost white
To burnt copper
Still as if lifeless
Or shaking like an Aspen in the fall

Beech Leaves Shimmer
From inside this bleak, dormant world
Announcing to those who are there and see

Winter is leaving
New life will push out last year's leaves

Spring is coming
On the verge of being green and vibrant once again

Endangered Numbered Days
by Candace R. Curran

He told me about New Zealand   flightless birds
living on island sanctuaries   owl-faced   soft-feather
rotund kakapo   ground dwellers disappearing
fewer than two hundred

and about the brilliance of orange-billed oystercatchers
waders with neon pink feet chasing in and out
back and forth in what seemed like
a pulse of endless waves

He told me he found himself in the bush
in the company of fantails   unknowingly
feeding them   turning up insects with
every step of his solo trek

and that he slept under a bright canopy
where tumbled stone and the silkies' ocean songs
washed clean and filled   heart
that jagged crag I opened

He said on his best days   in buoyant dreams
I was there with him   conjured in a berth he made
carried in a space he built   between wings
and not having wings

For the Whooping Crane
by Susan Marsh

Dark and silent reedgrass sloughs, coverts of cottonwood and ash

Buffaloberry embroidering a ditch with threads of crimson fruit.

October spreads its arms, waiting for the sky's embrace.

The land flattens under cumulus and growing light,

The blood-red line of sunrise broadens to a ruddy streak.

By noon the wind has turned, strong and from the north,

Primeval music tumbles from the vacant blue and all at once the sky fills

Angled rows of slender birds, wings like canvas sails,

Their hems dipped in ink. They disappear over the far bluffs

Horizons slanting away with the earth's broad curve.

Once we found beauty in their plumes, now in their rare flight.

The prairie sunset lingers, empty without cranes. This sky was made

For their thousands, its silence infused with their calls.

Twilight's fading violet settles into unforgotten pathways of air.

Tomorrow the sunrise will bleed again, the midday sky will wait

The only way it knows—arms open, ardent, filled with light.

N.B. *This poem was revised from the poem "Elegy for the Cranes," published in different form, with a different title, in the chapbook,* This Earth Has Been Too Generous, *by Finishing Line Press in 2022*

A Veil over Pendle.
by Julie Ross

Shades flicker beneath the trees that crown this hill, and the westering
sun gleams on emerald: the crown jewels are gold-green leaves,
whispering, and stirring in still air. Wild roses, blackthorn and whitethorn
circle its outer edge: the thorns are barbed and bent, the red and white
roses entwine, and the haw-snow falls, faerie pale. This hill lies in the land
of the Bow, beneath great Pendle the thrice named, the Ark that sails
through her Temple of the Stars. The zodiac is woven into the land here,
and around this very foothill pivot the feet of the Lion, the Bull, and
the Centaur, ever turning between the material world and faerie. This is
a meeting place for the crown and the feet, and it is a portal to Leithien,
the inner England of Tolkien's tales, that some call Albion.

But the Elves left long ago, and the Silmarils are lost to the material
world. Queen Arwen lies in the land, utterly forgotten by mankind.

Pendle and its inhabitants are deeply entwined with the Peace-Weaver.
The Lancashire mills lie desolate now, but for many years they were
an expression of her potency. She is the spinner, the weaver, and the
broiderer, whose arts are those of creation and metamorphosis, of
cosmic and individual destiny, where mind and matter are created,
measured, and recovered. I have seen Queen Arwen here, at the opening
hour. She ever spins the imperishable threads of Ea, that some call wyrd.
She ever weaves the fabric of the world, and ever stitches together the
kingdoms of faerie and man. She is the devoted one, the gift: she stitches
through the power of love, and in human form, she reminds us that we
too may adorn these designs. Here she dwells, hidden in plain sight, in
the deep Green, where spiral paths wind around this seventh stone, this
hollow hill. This is the white Castle, and if you stand here when white
clouds flee the south wind, and ragged crows ride the north wind, then
the Castle will turn.   For the veil is thin here.

For there is a gap in this crown, yawning, ever longing for the illusive
barrier between the worlds to close. But this Castle cannot be stormed:
it can be entered only by the blind path of the heart. Once inside, the
air shifts, and across the meadow are strewn inky shades of trees: the

enchanted tresses of Luthien released from their bonds. This is the deep Blue.

There are three portals here, and each one reveals a Silmaril, for those with eyes to see. They are guarded in the perilous realm, in once upon a time, each in an Elven crown etched into the landscape zodiac. The first appears via a straight road that runs from the cliff edge into the air: it cannot be seen but it can be trod. It passes through the seven glittering lights of the Bow and pierces the Virgin. It is the rainbow bridge of the Centaur, that forms the entwined crowns of Elwing, the white bird, and Eärendil, the radiant brow. This is the jewel in the sky.

The second reveals the golden crown of the Lion, which is the crown of Maglor the Bard, the foster-father. It is veiled in mist until the blackbird sings, when the mist rolls back to reveal the path that runs from crown of the Lion to its heart. Here meet the three Pendle rivers, Calder, Hodder and Ribble, only to mingle with starry waters from the cup of the Water-bearer. This is the jewel in the water.

The third unveils the crown of the great White Bull, who freely offers himself as a Gift. It can be seen from the cave, where the Seat of Seeing is situated. This is the crown of Maedhros the Tall, and is the crown of thorns, for his radiant light was revealed through a path of great torment. He has passed through the purification of fire; he is the bearer of the jewel at the heart of the Earth.

They were called the exiled, the dispossessed. But without them, the land too is dispossessed. And we are incomplete. So let me, too, sew, until the paths are restored, and the entwined crowns of Elves and Men blaze bright in the Blue-Green.

The Supernatural
by Georgia Gojmerac-Leiner

When sleepless I fled
to the Broadmoor Sanctuary
with outstretched arms I said,
"Take me in."
Then, as a spirit of nature
I moved among the forest denizens
over dry, uneven forest bed and
leafy undergrowth,
over brambles and scruffy pine,
over the beaten paths and the paths not taken,
over the beaver ponds and the vernal pools,
over mosses, fungi and lichen.
I knew these things in nature
as they know themselves;
I knew their silence;
I knew what it is like to be visible
yet overlooked.

Then, as when a pressure headache lifts,
a sense of well-being returned to me.
Now leaving the Sanctuary,
I moved through the trails with ease,
space parting before me
like the waters of Exodus.
Multicolored sparks bounced for gladness
as if juggled by tiny faery hands;
and in a cross-section of eroding soil,
whose layers, bearing fossils and genes,
tell the age of this corner of the universe,
I saw a myriad of varieties of life,
I saw myself as others will see me
hundreds or thousands of years hence,
when time has milled me
into a single particle—
and the vision gave me peace.

from Iona – A Sequence
by Victoria Field

Veil

They say the veil is thin here - perhaps
that's why I see the curly hair

of my unborn children unfurling
in the bracken, why my father

came to join us on the lawn
of the Argyll Hotel, lay down

on the daisies, beer in hand, why her
mother was spotted striding over

the golf course, her favourite song
audible on the wind. This veil is a kind

of tangible light, a scatter of sparkle,
hung between water and sky, the reason why

I keep catching the blackbird's yellow eye,
sense my grandmother passing my window at night.

Prayer

A black labrador's barking her prayers, bursts of love
from her doggy heart. Ferns on the nunnery wall

pray for roots and tenacity. Lambs bounce prayers of joy
over the tussocky turf of their world. Sheep, startled

by passers-by, piss their steaming streams of golden prayer.
The Abbey's prayer is ponderous with nineteenth century restoration.

A zigzag of medieval brickwork sings crazy prayers
in response. Bluebells shimmer their prayers.

Dandelions dot them along the verges. The black prayers
of rooks flap like burning paper in the few trees.

The concrete bin has a prayer engraved on its face,
'Litter Please' says its gaping mouth.

The prayers of the ancient carvings are silent,
smoothed by wind and time. Pilgrims pray with their smiles,

or don't with their chatter. All around, the sea prays like breath
in a circular pulse of hush and rush. The sun suddenly appears,

impatient, wants to show how it's done, gathers these prayers,
binds them tight, sends them all skyward in a pillar of light.

Ruined Nunnery

They're the loose women of the lawn,
dandelions, common and careless as sin,
not gilded like celandines,

untidy, putting it about, their yellow, a mad yellow,
tap roots, silly as stilettoes on a hen night,
anchoring them in rich dizzy grass,

mop-tops dense masses of little licks of flame.
Oh, every dandelion thinks she's the sun,
grins at the arrival of spring, coyly dips her shaggy head.

Dandelions speak dandelion, a wordless hum of yellow,
a spin of lion's teeth, soft suck of wet soil.
Dandelions have been here before,

listened to deliberations of nuns, prayer and plainsong,
seasoned their salads, made curious children pis-en-lit,
lived many lives in thin soil on old island's rock,

seams of serpentine greening their leaves.
Yet now they're new-born, blooming for the first time,
death, a buried rumour, nourishing their roots.

My own hair's metalling at the temples,
yellow fading to a fuzzy sphere of seeds.
When dandelions turn grey, it's all over,

they blow away, ride thermals into unbidden
winter. I have a sudden memory of lying in a field
with girlhood friends, in the early spring of our lives,

sharing the strangeness of first hairs sprouting
on our unblemished bodies, like weeds made of wire.
We'd shed our shoes and spin on the grass, faster

and faster, shaking our heads, playing the game
we called 'Dizzy', til we fell, aching with laughter
into the tussocky chaos of our future. Here, women's lives

were orderly, keeping daily offices, reading books of hours,
seasons held in place by feast days and festivals,
the silent ticking clocks of flowers.

Island

Every place is an island, every thing is an island.
All things that move, move round the island
or on the island, or under the island, or over the island
or through the island, or with the island, or next to the island
or a long, long, long, long way from the island.

The objects on the island are all islands:
the island of the abbey, the two hotels, the ruined convent.
The island of the road is a long, thin island made of tarmac.
The school is an island full of the cries of islands at play
The islands of the beaches, which abutt the island
are flooded twice daily by the island of the sea,
that vast doily with island-shaped holes cut into it.

There are rooted islands on the island, callled flowers and trees
There are flying islands on the island, called birds
There are woolly, unintelligent islands, standing all over the island,
called sheep.
The mountain on the island will soon, as sea levels rise, be an island.

I'm an island walking around the island.
I meet another island, he's wearing a tweed jacket and an island for a
hat.
He can name the rooted islands – dandelion, ransomes, sorrell
bluebells, those vast archipelagoes of blue islands.
I tell him the names of the flying islands – corncrake, rook,
curlew, song thrush spewing his islands of notes.

If sea levels weren't rising, he and I might have become
one island, a land mass even, or two islands
connected twice daily by a causeway. But he's more a star
than an island, becomes invisible in the noon day sun.

I take my island self off down the track, worry
I've misinformed him about the flying islands.
I really know nothing of islands nor the naming of islands.

N.B. Iona is a tiny island off the North West coast of Scotland, with a permanent population of around a hundred people. Every year, over three hundred thousand visitors make the complicated boat and bus journey there, drawn by the rich mix of Christian, Pagan and New Age associations, as well as the island's stunning natural beauty. Like many small, beautiful places, Iona has become packaged and, in some ways, a parody of itself. For me, it's an exemplar of the paradoxes inherent in our relationship to place. As human beings, we are often uncomfortable staying put. Some are forced to leave their land because of intertwined pressures of war, poverty, climate change and unsustainable agriculture. Others, myself included, with freedom to choose, travel to special places for personal growth or gratification. Having visited and enjoyed Iona, am I complicit in its degradation and even desecration?

Parts of this sequence have appeared in *A Speech of Birds* (Francis Boutle, 2020), *Hildegard Visions and Inspirations,* ed Gabriel Griffin (Wyvern Works, 2014), and *Scintilla 17*, 2014.

Immrama/Wanderings
by John Matthews

(Inspired by the ancient Irish tale of the Voyage of Maelduin)

The Isle of Voices

For days our keel
sliced through the black sea,
then suddenly before us
an island rising like a fist.
As we came to shore
drawn by the tide's secret hands,
we saw a crowd emerging from the rocks
who, when they saw us,
began to make such noise.
It was a while before we understood their words.
"It is they!" we heard, "It is they!"
Fear spread through us as we listened,
but before we could learn what this might mean
a wind sprang up, filling our sails,
and swiftly the island fell astern.
Yet it seemed we still could hear,
distant on the chill air:
"It is they, they, they!"

The Island of Laughter

The voyage was long, and we grew tired.
Then at noon we espied a new island,
a flat and grassy shore with low green hills
and distant clustering houses.
Along the shore and inland we could see
groups of fair people, laughing and dancing.
Eagerly, we pressed forward,
but caution ruled our captain
and only one, chosen by lot, we sent ashore.

Immediately he joined the play; he who had been,
a moment before, weary
and was, by nature, sad,
now gave vent to mirth and pleasure.

In wonder we watched him,
greeting folk as though he knew them well,
and felt the sorrow of those
who know too much of laughter.

Grimly we turned our craft about
and left the shore and our fellow
to what we thought must be
unending merriment. Behind us,
as dusk fell, we heard laughter and shouting still,
that followed us on the clear air.

The Island of God's Trees

On the next island we met a man,
ancient as care, who told us how,
when a youth, he had set sail,
following the sea's green road
in search of God. But his boat
had begun to tremble, though the sea
remained flat calm, and so returning
to land, he cut four squares of turf
to steady the rocking of his craft.

Thereafter he sailed on easily
until, reaching this spot
on the open sea, his boat
would sail no further.
Then, God himself appeared
(the old man could give us
no description)
and set the strips of turf
side by side on the open sea.

'Each year since then,'
he told us with pride,
'God has added
another foot to this island;
and with each foot a tree;
and in each tree are birds -
the souls of those who died
after I left the shores of my country.
These God himself sends to me.'

We smiled among ourselves at this,
but the old man seemed harmless,
and next day, after we had eaten,
taking care not to disturb
the birds that roosted in the trees,
we left his island and sailed on -
only once looking back
to watch it sink quietly in mist.

The Island of Youth

The third from last island
at the end of the world
was green and shadowed deeply with trees.
There the fabled unicorn ran free
and maidens fairer than jewels
came offering fruit and wine;
and in a pool of clear water
where we bathed,
those who were aged found youth again.

Long days we spent there,
Lost to the voyage, 'til one morning,
inexplicably, the dream passed
like a shiver across the skin,
and we woke on our ship once more,
water sliding beneath its lively keel.

Five Poems
written by Yuan Hongri
translated by Yuanbing Zhang

Cherish: The Memory of the Heaven

Today I would like to thank the world that looks like the hell.
It makes the fire that cherish the memory of the Heaven burning inside
me;
it reminds me of the precious fruit of the sweet golden tree.
Those palaces and towers swirling music from outer space,
those giants whose bodies are limpid and happy,
those oceans are blue cocktails,
those rivers are the nectar of the soul;
However those mountains float in the sky like clouds, layer upon layer.
None of stone has no transparent smile.
The wind pass through the body and sings mysterious words.
None of flowers will wither,
as if old sun is both eternal and young.

怀念天堂

今天 我想感谢这地狱的人间
它让我体内燃起怀念天堂的火焰
让我回忆起甜蜜的黄金之树的宝石之果
那飘洒着天外乐曲的宫殿楼阁
那身体空明而欢喜的巨人
那海洋是蓝色的鸡尾酒
那河流是灵魂的琼浆
而那山岳如云朵般飘浮
在层层叠叠的天际
没有一块石头没有透明的笑容
风穿过身体吟唱 神秘的词语
没有一朵花会凋谢
仿佛古老的太阳 永恒而年轻

Don't Forget The Other You

Don't forget the other you,
those numerous yous, either in the body or outer space,
those sweet smiles and the diamond flowers that never wither,
that make boundless years on earth turn into a snippet of bird song.
Yes, the crows of a heavenly Phoenix.
Those sweet lightnings hit you,
let you suddenly wake up and see Gold Heaven is with you.
And your body is the golden body of giants,
and makes all time become sweet.

不要忘了那另一个你

不要忘了那另一个你
那在身体里在天外的众多的你
那甜蜜的笑容永不凋谢的钻石之花
让你在尘世的漫漫岁月化成一声鸟鸣
是的，那是天国鸾凤的啼鸣
那甜蜜的闪电击中了你
让你恍然醒来 看见黄金的天国与你同在
而你的身体是巨人的黄金之体
让一切时光变得甜美

Never-withering Light

I can't say the mystery of the gods yet,
the devil is coveting the diamond of heaven.
There is a golden kingdom whose light is like wine inside the ancient
earth.
The smiles of the gods are beside you,
as if they are the rounds of invisible sun and moon.
And your soul is ancient and holy
twinkles with the never-withering light of stars.

不凋谢的光芒

我还不能说出那诸神的奥秘
魔王在觊觎天国的钻石
在这古老的大地的体内
有那光芒如酒的金色王国
诸神的笑容就在你身旁
仿佛一轮轮隐形的日月
而你的灵魂也古老神圣
闪烁辰星那不凋谢的光芒

My Heaven is Inside My Body

My heaven is inside my body,
my heaven is a great many,
like stars in the night sky,
with silver towers,
huge edifices that look like sapphires,
golden palaces, gardens of crystal.
My body is bigger than the universe,
countless gods and angels are my partners,
as if they are countless myself.
Neither time nor life and death in my words,
dawn and dusk are the same name,
and sadness and joy are the same words.

我的天国在身体之内

我的天国在身体之内
我的天国居多犹如夜空的繁星
白银的楼阁　蓝宝石的巨厦
黄金的殿堂　水晶的花园
我的身体比宇宙更巨大
无数的天神与天使是我的伙伴
他们仿佛是无数的我自己
我的词语里没有时间也没有生死
黎明与黄昏是同一个名字
而悲伤与欢喜是同一个词语

The Hymn of Sweet Soul

Drape the night over my shoulders like a cloak of the world,
call the birds of the stars from outer space and fly near my city garden.
Sing a song of the giants from huge city of platinum,
awoke the drowsy city of the world with a start.
Oh, the lightnings are in full bloom in the vault of heaven —the hymns of
sweet soul.
Your bones became transparent suddenly,
its light was flickering all over the body like the wings,
in a flash, the body became huge, higher than the large building
down the street.

那甜蜜灵魂的圣歌

把黑夜披在肩上如一件世界之斗篷
召唤天外的星辰之鸟飞临我的城市花园
唱一曲白金巨城的巨人之歌
惊醒这昏沉的人间之城
哦 闪电在天穹盛开 那甜蜜灵魂的圣歌
你的骨骼骤然透明 光芒如翅翼在周身闪烁
一刹那身体巨大 高过了街边的巨厦

This Is Our Fate
by Maria Perez

We're all clinging onto ideas of life that are too small to hold
Wishing the story of infidelity that once stained our soul can be untold
The crashing tidal waves in our mind are not enough to wake us from our
slumber
The icy cold water only makes us more numb and dumber
The bitter taste that fills our lungs when we drown makes us become
more
deficient
Defenseless and restless the flame of purpose serves as our reminiscent
I feel as though I am still sleeping when I am very much awake
I'll do anything to feel less delusional when my sanity is at stake
I'll draw blood from my wrist so this nightmare can lift
I'll crack my own vessel to be sure I exist
The pain will snap my lethargy in two
Would you believe me if I told you there was nothing else I could do?
I am clinging onto ideas of life that are too small to hold
But the roots of suffering beneath my skin blossom so that my heart may
unfold

Who To Blame?
by Maria Perez

Ambiguity blooms as she walks
She walks with death holding one hand and time holding the other
How unfair it is when she has so much left on earth to discover
Still there was a balance set when she had the chance to take her first
breath
All her outcomes of complications were determined by her strength
Would it be the fault of her own if she no longer wanted to keep
walking?
Would the reasons she held onto in order to stay, be infinite, even if she
isn't?
Would she find what lies on the other side if she persists to exist?
Or could she be mindlessly chasing answers that were never there?
There's hypocrisy in her heart when she pretends to not care
Yet at night her thoughts whisper the truth she did everything to avoid
Tell me is it the fault of her own if she was wired by the devil to be
toyed?
Or did she create the devil herself to blame someone else for her sins
Unpredictability excites her from within
Even if she knew her ending is permanent no matter how many times
her story begins

fire song
by Suzanne S. Rancourt
—July 2020, for Uncle Dale

when fire combusts, bark shudders a fluttering sound
a low tone of small wings beating
reds, oranges, with black under wings, underbelly
the hardwood has not yet turned to grey ash
maybe this is what the scarlet tanager heard?
this sound of distress, battle or love, and was overcome by desire
incessant need to fly into the feathering flame's center
that ruffled steady for eight days and welcomed
this bird that did not question why
it had to touch the fire and rose in rapid back strokes
tail feathers already black, already singed
rising
riding
a water dome of flames

and why not?
by Suzanne S. Rancourt

didn't miss the jets flying over head during the inevitable
pandemic and quarantine
Earth does not need us - we need her

squirrels monkeyed their acrobatic stealth
creatures came closer today
that Osprey flew up the trail from the spring
glided 20 feet – settled silently on a hemlock branch
just like i'd dreamt 30 years ago
that's the raptor petroglyph tattoo
incised on my back - shoulder to shoulder
aligned specifically with sinew, bone, cartilage
with every shoulder roll, i fly

the salmon in my eye is not an iris
by Suzanne S. Rancourt

it is an arched rainbow
repousse – curved in relief
cats crescent bodies and tail
a simple spiral chase
jump steps upstream
cats & fish- water & wind
earth & sky – this soul salmon
undulates rivers oppositional eroticism
prerecorded instructions
single mindedness their focus tethered
filament hooked into survival
spawn
bear all
because splayed honesty
is everything dignity tells

you are yelling from your yawning mouth
from the opposite shore watching me
ridge runner paces waiting for that thing
that thing you say is there for me to do
the salmon in my eyes are caught
in arching kick propulsion
like mosquito larvae or snapping white fly squiggles
in the potted plants we water
i convulse my future
regardless

everything has already happened, my job is to show up
by Suzanne S. Rancourt

The only one making stew on a wood cookstove
where I keep putting my stocking feet into the oven to warm up
I'm certain I smell aromatic carrots and beef wafting across this porch
even the Hawk that maneuvered its 1 meter wingspan along the trail
stopped just short of the railing, eyeballing me
I sat quiet 'cause I ain't nobody but a guest here and
anyone who stays for more than a couple a days needs checking out.

Blue jays got nervous for the squirrels, chipmunks & such
& sent their point man to zero in on Hawk's back as he/she
flew a sneak-up 'round the red squirrel condo.
This female Jay struck hard enough to count coup
& the Hawk took off but not before a glance back
& we understood sometimes just showing up instigated an attack
even here in the woods
just because we are who we are.

I get it Hawk man or woman. I get it too Bear person.
Those ferns undulate a riffle that chipmunks' tight chirp rings steady
hunting down from the sky, out from behind clouds,
boomerang bones & clamping talons swipe up the scurrying.

I'm sipping tea like some Attenborough show or
that ancient Marlin Perkins – even ravens have swallowed their croaks
I keep smelling beef stew & wonder
if that big black bear snorting around the cabin
sucking in my scent from between the unchinked logs smells it too

we have to leave home to want home
for a long time I wasn't sure where home was

I remember warm feet, biscuits, stew.

A Scab of Heat
by Suzanne S. Rancourt

the afternoon, incandescent in humidity
a light flutters the mosquito netting
ripples, dips down from the open sun umbrella

the afternoon when sun crosses the roof's
equatorial apex, latches onto the west
it is in this time that I can get lost

drinking hot espresso wondering what are the turkeys
clucking about, maybe, i was whistling
to the hawks again

hitch onto their continuum like the 100 foot
orange garden hose, soft now
hot & fat from late august sun

to be still without guilt, to crave the hawks' whistle
it is difficult not to move instead
count the ravens' caw

locations – the fisher dug up the ground hornets' nests
ate them returned night after night
gorging on hornet impertinence and tenacity

how fitting to be alone feasting
on the elements of presence, acceptance,
the luxury of beauty

Ashes to Ashes
by Sharon Harmon

Building slash piles
in the woods
bending to broken limbs
we haul and drag, pile and stash

our muscles stretch in fluid motion
limbs become extensions
of gnarled root bound undergrowth
woodsy moss, ferns and powdery

mushrooms leave a decaying
dirt odor in the air; ashes to ashes
leaves to dust
at the ends of our lives

we recycle our bodies
never ending resurrection
transgressions and souls,
mired into cool silent forests

Hiking to Chapel Falls
by Libby Maxey

We come and go, the journey of an hour
or two, an afternoon, not seasonal,
not necessary. Frail, the small wildflower
of our ambition fades before the full
expression of a monarch's blooming need,
a bobolink's unquestionable charge
to cover continents. And yet the weed
of our well-homed complacency grown large
on little wonder snaps a juicy green
in unexpected teeth. Along the trail
we meet a goat, so tame and plump and clean
she might have spoken. Lost, she seeks the grail:
her fellows and their grain, their lenient pen.
We lead her home where we have never been.

Land of the Old Boatman
by Chandra Gurung

Dil Bahadur Majhi, an old boatman
Rows his days on the surface of the Narayani
Enjoys in the village of its water
Roves along its aquatic streets
Devoid of color
Devoid of taste
Devoid of form
Lives a life like that of water

The papers come quite early in the morning
Carrying news of the chaos in the nation
The old radio hung from the roof of his hut
Airs, in crackling sound, the news of disorder.
Dil Bahadur Majhi sighs in exhaustion
Raising his wrinkled forehead higher
And prints, all over his heart
The images of those who cross the deep Narayani
To move to countries far-off
Carrying homes and families in their eyes
And the nation in their hearts

Here the town-squares honk their dissent
And the streets call for a shutdown
Many lives have gone away
Crossing the Narayani of misery
In such difficult time
Dil Bahadur scribbles on his canvases
The ripe eyes tending lonely homes
The incomplete honeymoons waiting for youthful nights
The guiltless cheeks that covet a father's kiss

Standing alone on the bank of the Narayani
Dil Bahadur Majhi stares—
At several dejected porters moving town-ward;
At several needy lives moving across the border.

In the fish net of musings, he snares—
The cheap deals of blood and sweat that spill abroad
The paradoxical reverberation of the slogan 'Aayo Gorkhali'
In a war in an alien land
And the darkness of a red-light area in Mumbai

Like in the chest of the old boatman
This country aches in hearts
Countless in number

Portage from Canoe lake to Tom Thomson lake
by Robert Fleming

right palm part of paddle
elbow tips in 2 Algonquin park lake
stroke & stroke
camp counselor orders paddles up
portage ahead
canoe bow on half sand, half dirt
& counselor orders
stop digging ur blade in the sand
empty the canoe
counselor worse than father?
put this pack on your back
& follow the trail, tree marked yellow –
counselor worse than 2 carry?
up, Up, UP, a hill
Down dOwn down my back
pack, a flat, Ups and dowNs
& i dodge a snake
but fall in 2 a pond
counselor worse than wet pack?
canoe stern on half dirt, half sand
campers as you enter the canoe,
put ur paddle across the thwart
as the canoe pushes off the sand
my right palm becomes part of the paddle grip
my left palm becomes part of the paddle throat
campers we have completed the

Portage from Canoe lake to Tom Thomson lake

Costa da Morte
by Mary Brancaccio

And he said unto them, take me up, and cast me forth into the sea; so shall the sea be
calm unto you: for I know that for my sake this great tempest is upon you.
—Jonah 1.12

Salvation is a bitter seed, a thin coat
against driving rain, an ache for years lost
a sapphire sea beautiful and treacherous.

Northern winds fill my ears with muted roar
as I hike through spiky camariños
past an English cemetery to a beach.

I walk on unmarked sand, in spirit steps
of those whose shipwrecked lives were birthed here.
One hundred-fifty years ago, three sailors

swam ashore in a tempest from the dying Serpent
to claim a second life as nine-score drowned.
I imagine each man, sodden and cold

bare feet on prickly nettles, stunned into silence
each convinced that he alone survived,
until word spreads of other walking English.

Knitted joy and despair as they met up
where Fes de Deus, dozens of stone cairns
testify to casualties on the wild Atlantic.

I port my pilgrim heart in open view.
Let me atone for my dead, for loved ones
lost. My past is a broken hull.

The Calling
by Yehudit Silverman

I have to
lean into longing
like a pilgrim
whose hands are empty

Only wind
and perhaps the whisper
of a cellular calling
I never asked for

A child held tight
by secrets
a corset
no breath

No becoming
the wilderness
that grows unbidden
between ribs
between lips
between pilgrim and prayer

You look at my long robe
and see starlight
as if I can lead you
easily
through the dark
as if my feet
don't bleed
as they open

Tell me
how to be
in this wild walking

how to feel the flight
of all things lifted

tell me...

The Angel of Chartres
by James Harpur

A fierce breeze tries to shove me back
inside the train; but I resist and glide
through sun-buffed, littery streets,
cathedral towers playing hide and seek
as I turn a corner here, there, recalling
Rodin and Rilke arriving on a winter's day,
Rodin abusing Chartres's gothic scowls,
Rilke scarfed against the sleet of words,
the east wind embittering his eyes,
and his life in flux, marriage flailing;
and Rodin still relentless in his grousing
until they turn the corner I now turn
and all at once we see the angel,
the slender angel low down on the wall
who's holding out an offering:
a semi-circle of stone, a sundial
dissolving time to a stick of shadow
that's poised like a fishing float poised
to pull quicksilver life from flux
and if only for a moment tear
the spirit from the body
and raise it high

        shimmering

and wriggling

       into the element of air.

Lucid Journey: June 2020
by Diana Hirst

Vegetation, luminous in morning sun,
green and lush, young and bouncy
as a puppy dog, licking me all over,
is rampant, overwhelming even apple trees.
It drives me through the six-foot wooden door
in the high wall of iron-red bricks and crumbly mortar.
Fearful of its exuberance, I take a final glimpse
before I close the door, and slide the bolt decisively.

This place is dark and dank and damp;
the ground slopes steeply down
to murkiness that reeks of ancient cess pits.
No path is evident through knotted undergrowth.
Brittle broken twigs and brambles,
their thorns aggressive, forbid passage.
This cannot be a *bois dormant*:
it is the stuff of nightmares, not of fairy-tales.

*****

The Sainsbury trolley had been half-concealed
by brambles weaving through its wire frame.
But its orange handle's visible and free,
a welcome beacon in this foetidness.
I seize it, tweak it, twist it.
It still has wheels, so I can push
a battering ram through the undergrowth
to force my exit from this place.

Brittle twigs give way before this Juggernaut,
they cling to my hair, snag on my clothes.
My feet crunch on detritus,
my legs and arms seep blood.
Two yards are cleared, then five, then ten:
I burst through dead vegetation

to where once there was a path.
A metal barrier stops me crashing in a road.

The world out here is tarmac-grey,
anonymous. Where to now?
Right looks purposeful, still grey
but curving down towards a lighter place.
Off-white kerb stones edging
anodyne grey pavement mark out a trail
past bungalows crouching behind low walls,
refusing to communicate.

*****

As the trail slopes and curves,
familiar gull cries and a growing rumble-rhythm
spark recognition that the air's moving more freely.
I sniff expectantly. There is the sea!
My dear Thalassa glimmers beneath a clouded sun.
Quickening my step, kicking off my shoes,
I run across the sand to bathe my crusting scabs
in her salty healing water.

The sky has bands of yellow
stretched taut above the horizon.
One by one Thalassa gathers them,
pleats them to herself.
In the onshore evening breeze,
transforming them to white,
she releases them to shore.
Bubbling whiteness nibbles my feet.

*****

Large irregular flints pave my uphill way
till I reach the orchard
in its evening crepuscule.
Here the morning's rampant grass is mown and lies in windrows,

ready to be turned for winter's hay.
The apple trees stand, their dignity restored,
glossy green leaves above the grey knurled trunks:
the June drop lying at their roots.

In the ancient wall, the door stands flush,
no bolt or handle on this side, just a escutcheon.
Beside the door, above some ragstone steps
a panel reads 'Stairs leading to Dorter'.
As I stand at their foot, ready to ascend,
from its lookout at the top of a telegraph pole
a blackbird bugles snatches of *The Gay Gordons*,
to signal it will soon be 'Lights Out'.

Travel Log
by Charles Perrone

"Oh my God!" you exclaim
—and good day by the way—
your former de-filing and claim (Re:)
your ancient excavation, revindication
has been lost ir-
regardless (of) your efforts
and furtive fortifications of the lot;
despite all care in the air (de, ir, etc.)
to fare well where no man has before,
to forge no manifold control,
to make some trio, two, or one
happy in a holding pattern,
to stay content, to accept the content at a distance,
safe-sexed-unhexed-and-free of all numeric takes,
full-noun explanations of destinies and / or sorts,
(lucks, locks, licks, lacks of lexical coherence)
hic et nunc, here and now, what do you expect?:
you're past the security check, frightful threshold,
you've asked (to be answered) if it's always this tight
and passed into the night, full of fear, full of life.

Phoenix Farm: Midnight, May 29, 2022
by Michael Carey

as its end approached
the phoenix fashioned a nest
of aromatic boughs
and spices, set it on fire,
and was consumed in the flames
              —Encyclopedia Britannica

No sun, no moon, no stars,
even thought dissolves
in darkness, within darkness
within darkness.

No sound save
the wind whispering
its secrets to the evergreens
who scatter them like seeds
all around me and through
the surrounding fields.

The sky is covered
by motionless clouds
even though I know
both I and the clouds
are moving
through the universe
at mind-boggling speeds
and in many directions
we have never been before
all at once.

The wind blows me
to the brightness,
of heavenly truth
that is everywhere
in everything.

Oh, if tomorrow is granted me
I will watch for it again,
and every tomorrow after that,
because deep in the future
my soul is following me around
reminding me of now,
where inside layer
upon layer of darkness,
a faint orange glow begins
to permeate the heavens
with promise, with new life
out of yesterday's ashes,
a new beginning,
a new sun,
a new agriculture,
slowly spreading
its enormous
wings over us.

Phoenix Farm, November 2021
by Michael Carey

I

One after another, houses ride
the high undulations of the land
like wooden ships looking for
the promise of a safe harbor.

II

Silently, a hawk hovers above us
allowing, for the time being,
an updraft to hold it in mid-air until it
pulls in its wings and plummets headfirst
in what seems a suicidal frenzy
picking up speed and momentum
until, a few inches from the ground, its wings
shoot out and its beak smashes the skull
of a small unwary rabbit which it then picks up
in its talons and struggles to fly away with.

III

God, I love the fall,
the multitudinous shades of brown,
and red, and green, all the crops,
dry and ready, standing straight
in gently curving rows
waiting to bear their gifts
of rest from constant worry
and never-ending labor, making room
in its farmers' brief lives
for a safe and secure Christmas.

IV

We are strangers here, but my Irish wolfhound
immediately feels at home running wildly
in joyful figure eights and circles
telling me, in no uncertain terms, that like me,
he too, in a previous life, was a farmer.

But this land is different.
I've never seen so many trees planted on crop ground,
their roots faithfully holding its soil in place.
No erosion here, or tonnage of chemical poison.

V
Whoever said Iowa is flat and all its roads are straight
has never steered through and around
these beautiful hidden hills outside Morse,
five miles northeast of Iowa City.
Think the rounded Grant Wood landscape
around Stone City, the tilted tableland
hiding countless round bales of hay
waiting to be punctured by large tines
attached in the rear to a tractor's three-point hitch,
then lifted and stored in a huge grassy mountain
to become, months later, much-needed feed
for wintering livestock. As the road curves,
a large herd of cattle and sheep appear
out of what, a moment ago, you assumed
an empty landscape. Here, the miraculous
is common to those who notice.

All morning, the raised augers of red and green combines
pour the fruits of endless labor into trucks and wagons
to provide against the long white winter
everyone knows is coming.

VI
Afternoons such as this remind me
that Earth is a heavenly body,
as are all who live upon it, heavenly
bodies full of heavenly bodies,
and that no matter what we do to it,
or have done, or will do, it will go on,
one way or another, with or without us.

In Praise of the Smallest Creatures on the Fourth Largest Island in
America
~*Whidbey Island, Washington*

By Heidi Seaborn

Let your feet settle into the sand's hold. Behold
the pom poms of purple sea urchins, barnacled
goose-neck mussels bubbling gently in a nest of seaweed.
A pale pink sea star puffs on a rock, while crabs scurry out
and the green anemone wave their tentacles and suck
whatever the tide washes into their sand-crested mouths.

Crouch down in the drainage ditch. Go no further.
There on the edge of civilization, a long-toed salamander,
a garter snake. A red-legged frog eyes the skitter bugs,
a painted turtle emerges from the grass and damsels
spin through the buttercups and iris. And now a rail lands
with a slight flap of wings, disturbing things.

Haven't we disturbed so much to see the big picture,
to get the panoramic shot? On an island of vistas
reaching past the horizon, we swoon for sunsets,
for the sweep of storms, for high bluffs and suspension
bridges. Binoculars trained on the orcas, the bald eagle.
Always the pursuit of big, bigger, biggest.

But note the ants nosing the trail, the beetle. For every rustle
in the grass, there is a story. Let the longhorn bee tell you
of foxglove and hairy vetch. Listen to the hummingbirds
in the cluster rose, hear the rush of ryegrass, the creep of lichen,
the quiet shift as the water parts for marbled murrelet.
Watch the orbweaver dangle from an ash branch.

Remain close to ground in praise of the wild of Whidbey Island.

Ode to Whidbey Island
by Heidi Seaborn

O the shape of you—the final
puzzle piece carved by ice—
like a human pulling knees in, kicking
heels away into an aperçu.

To arrive at your feet by ferry,
to travel the curved highway of your spine
to the high bridge crossing the turquoise
whirlpools swirling the head of you.

O the wild and tame body of you like the doe
sauntering slowly across the village road.
The succulent you—Penn Cove mussels steamed
and spicey at the bar in Toby's Tavern.

The green bramble of you, summer air
dusty with the scent of blackberries and silly
with children's singsong along your necklace
of beaches, tented with driftwood forts.

O the dark wooded thicket of you, needled
and nettled, cedar and fir. O feathered hills.
Old farmhouses haybale the meadows,
perch like eagles overlooking bays.

The bays: O Mutiny, Useless,
Honeymoon. The wind of you,
the weather of you. And look, O Canada!
O the orcas, the chase of salmon.

The sludgy low tide of you, pungent
with seaweed and barnacled with grounded boats.
The swell of multi-million-dollar beach homes.
The strip malls: O Oak Harbor.

O the history, the bloody history
of you. The explorers. Manifest Destiny.
Relics of wars fought & won & still to come—
O hear the fighter jets' deep-throated roar.

Whidbey Island, I have camped on
your bluffs as the sun tilted over the Salish Sea,
walked the shoulders of your beaches, sailed
your waters, eaten mussels, clams & crab.

O I've feasted from your fields & cycled
your backroads furred with scotch broom
& Queen Anne's lace. O Whidbey, to sleep once
more beneath your eternal reach of stars.

Refuge
by Jeri Theriault

You start in the parking lot overlooking
the football field of your old school
cross the street   pass the new condos

and enter the leaf-shadowed place
you heard about for the first time
yesterday. Moss-muted   sun

aloof   just you and the turtles and
chipmunks   traffic noise a burr
at the edge of consciousness

low bird sounds—chitter and wing flap.
The pond ripples. Exploded cattails
and grasses wave in the small breeze.

Eastern white pines filter light
rustle and moan   understory
undergrowth   decomposing stumps

one pine over-turned   its roots forced
into air   wood duff churned
by scurrying   everything a lesson—

we all go back to particle and speck—
while saplings   Canadian mayflowers
fiddleheads   raise green questions

amid the x's of tangled roots
whatever seeds   whatever comes
curated by the unwritten rules

of sun and damp and chance.
You sit still for a long time
with the chirps and plops

woodpeckers and spring peepers
in this place you feel you should know—
gray-green chapel—no   not chapel

with its bible and dominion—
only burrow or lair   place
of shadow   song and air.

Creation Story
by Jeri Theriault
　　　Dow's Woods 2022

Blanding's Turtle　small armored mother
lays eggs near blacktop where humans
leave bitter & unbreakable cup lids
wrappings　all manner of plastic

their words & noise & taking. Turtle makes
her nest　low-down & solid　goes about
what she goes about—hibernates　basks
estivates—in the duff　the dirt

the welcome damp　her natural span
seventy years. She goes on as long
as she can　the earth balanced
as always　on her back

Walking Tour
by Jeri Theriault
           South Portland ME, 2022

From Dow's Woods I walk down Highland
to Boothby and slip from sidewalk
to Trout Brook's rooty path
under pines and maples
this wild understory written
by woodchucks   moles

and skunks   all edged by fence   wood pile
and lawnmower. Sawyer St. marsh
then wild grass   bamboo and milkweed
at the end of Broadway. Bug Light—
where I watch ferries   container ships
and yachts.

Shore walk   for a glimpse of open sea
and big sky—white sails and American Airlines
coming in. Everything overlaps—
backyards   giant oil tanks
and the tidal flats near Hannaford's
with ducks and gulls

and sometimes a great blue heron. Fox
in my backyard   three baby raccoons
and strutting turkeys. Blue jay
and squirrel   little mother turtle   invasive
forsythia   trail-running boy   you
with the leaf blower

and you with your tomato seedlings
and *Bee Safe* sign   all of us the fabric
of this place. Even the blacktop
with its roadkill and bicycle
danger   ties us   mostly   together
takes us away and brings us home again

atomic theory 7 — poems to my wife and God
by Shann Ray

even the dark is not dark
to you or the night-blooming
hypnotic-scented cereus

even night is as the day we first met

we sometimes encounter avulsion
grinding compression
by weight by steel wheels passing
over chest and limbs lead metal and glass
tearing the skin the margins irregular uneven

yet we were married in a single knowing
light quantum borne in electrons
at night networks of stars and a breath
her instep touched to my calf the arch of her
ribs your handiwork in my hands

vii.1

light is more contained less fractured
in healthy cells light are your kisses o God
light are the kisses of your mouth
harmonize us o marry us
to each other to the world and you

we drop fire bombs followed by atomic wounding
among the thousand-fold wounding from which we never recover

in your memory we are no longer at war here or overseas
the city a melody like mountain blue jays humming
over sylvan lake let him kiss me with the kisses she says
of his mouth for your love is wine

mystic and east rosebud in the beartooth range
where the absaroka wilderness sets the yellowstone
north to the missouri then south to the gulf of mexico

vii.2

we want to be done
with cutting and killing ourselves
we want to usher the beast into and out of our hearts
i believe we are all abandoned
all loved

immanuel means God with us and we burn like stars

crippled hydrogen atoms no longer absorb or emit light
but can be resurrected by choice

deep tissue unevenly divided
foreign bodies in the wound
a curved laceration made of rock or water
the skin torn free or undermined
blood is life that's why we carry small stones in our pockets
and set them in the vault of heaven

vii.3

cut edges are normally clean

length greater than width the wound usually

spindle shaped leaving more blood on the long plain before the great
mountains

where the genocided women walk with lanterns alongside those who
delivered genocide

women and men loved whole in the house made of dawn

your miracles reside in montana and in the bedroom where momaday
sleeps

everyday i see my cousin jacine and my brother and me holding hands

over the river the summer before she died jacine wore the shirt of flame

so did charlie calf robe paul deputy and bobby jones who hung himself

while the other three were shot or bludgeoned to death and i said we all
wear

the shirt of flame and my teacher said some more than others some so
much more

how is it i was deeply loved by them i still don't know

the motherless empty the fatherless hungry dismay so dark in my
jawbone

o God that's why i cry into the wooden bowl of my hands

vii.4

clubbing instruments cause skull fractures fissured depressed
comminuted
the skull inbuckled the bones broken in several places
near here is the town where children were gassed to death or burned in
industrial ovens
human bodies burn readily the hands and feet drop off under sudden
intense heat
all men young and old in broad daylight three bullets each head chest
chest murder

in the house of dawn which is your house
on a long hill outside prague your miracles hidden in roses
symphonic atoms rosettes of nuclear light in the wrist bones of those
dead in the garden

of friendship and peace in the shadows where the children of my
grandmother's massacred ones
hold hands with the children of those who massacred them
my children of peace with me my children of war planting
a hundred thousand roses again o wounds of God with us always
my God Christ where is my wife where are my children

vii.5

—*for Marie Uchytilová*

dear God our nameless one
we love our daughters and sons
but do not let us forsake our fathers

o name above all names
let us love them with electromagnetic gravitational force
for forsaking them we forsake ourselves each father understood
as the dynamics of a field the cut is deeper at entry due to greater
pressure
the head leads to the tailing a blade entered obliquely bevels one edge
at the other's expense for atomic life absorbs light
but a horizontal blade causes a flap wound

o let us love them

Lord let us go to them with joy in our eyes
preparing them for death by asking forgiveness and by forgiving them
their tritium boosting their double yield so they can die knowing we love
them

vii.6

you sense us she and i brought to blossom

with you we don't live by ourselves
and we don't die alone either

beauty like smoke through the doorway
of worlds beyond division we die with each
other and happily the images we make of you are nothing
compared to the bodies you give us
light waves loops and strings light bullets
portable never-ending o numinous *mysterium tremendum*
et fascinans et flame the ultimate danger
fear-invoking fear-transcending merciful compassionate
your touch the press of my hand to her forehead and hips
the zenith of her ribs her curved bones set over
the opening you made for the infinite

vii.7

—*for Rudolf Otto*

in the beginning
a burden of water a veil of light
the word was a cyclone at the edge of the eye

a chop wound a blow with the cutting end of a heavy instrument
an axe a butcher knife a machete a sword
the margins sharp and deep john the son of thunder said the weak
interaction
is radioactive decay is essential the word was love was light was God
essential nuclear fission and fusion with God all things came into being

apart from God nothing came into being

the word a continuous range of electromagnetic gravitational energy

heat color light of the snail's nautilus
o crown rack of bull elk the neckline the life cluster
and edible thistle blue iris foxteeth boxwood and blue-eyed grass
the light shines in a darkness the darkness cannot comprehend
cannot overcome

vii.8

our mothers are your mother
with sacred heart ablaze
and my father as he moves through ancient mountains

fir and lodgepole above clear rivers below black skies

you the storm we flee the storm we return to
rainsoaked running the gorge
at pine creek in the beartooth wilderness where lightning rings
from canyon walls and our mouths eat fire

the magnitude of your love still frightens us

i've met too many old pale men who say Christ
is with them but treat their mothers ugly
their wives and daughters and other women along with their country

the velocity of light is 186,000 miles per second

the gravitational force attracts anything with mass

vii.9

but blessed are those who listen
to the poverty of wildflowers
and find night so near dawn

over a dismembered animal
bears still remember the bugle bloom
about to shout and how penetrating
wounds puncture the body cavity

tissue and muscle
sinew and joints and bone

but unlike bears we forget how the night shines
we go about forgetting the force manifest
in electric fields magnetic fields
and light marsh hollyhock buttonweed redstem storksbill
fated by need we hastily imprint violence

vii.10

—for Louise Erdrich and
Mary Oliver

in the darkness she and i thank you
and we listen to each other so now that we're older
she still presses her face to mine
and i still lay my head on her chest asking her as we die
where are you going hearing her say i'm going to God

where what is least familiar is most named
and what is most sublime is least comprehended

at night i cup my hand to the back of her head the line of her jaw
our worldskin a dark conflation of night and light
so when she looks into me i see you
the body the city trillium deer's-head orchid fawn lily

with my name hidden she draws herself over me
and kisses me and we both soon slumber

your beauty our night all light

vii.11

N.B. *These 11 sonnets first appeared in* Bearings, *and were published in the collection of poems* atomic theory 7 – poems to my wife and God *(Resource Publications)*

Möbius

by Cynthia Anderson

> ...*we were not born to survive*
> *Only to live*
> —W. S. Merwin

You imagine a point of no return.
But it's not there—it's not anywhere—

despite the grudges you carry
or your fading body. You learn this

as you stand in the warm sun,
watching the effortless circles

of turkey vultures, a blackened kettle
ballooning and flattening, a sky snake

coiling and uncoiling—soaring
on thermals, wheeling northward,

splitting and regrouping, closer
and farther, until they are smaller

than sparrows, then gone—
a surge in the tide of migrants

who will be back before you know it,
tracking the scent of death,

surprising you as they did today
with an arrival out of season—

urging you to turn
from your scavenging on earth

toward the mystery of flight.

Poet and Translator Index

Artist Index

Poem Index

R

S

T, U

V

W, X

Y, Z

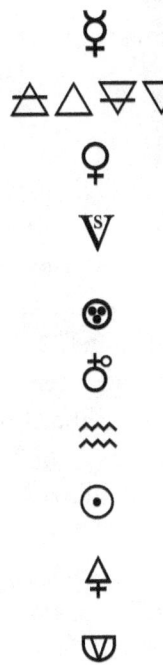

Poets', Translators', and Artists' Biographies

Cynthia Anderson has published 12 poetry collections, most recently *Arrival* (Sheila-Na-Gig Editions, 2023) and *Full Circle* (Cholla Needles Press, 2022). Her poems appear frequently in journals and anthologies, and her work has been nominated for the Pushcart Prize and Best of the Net. She has lived in California for over 40 years. "Möbius" was first published in *Waking Life, Poems by Cynthia Anderson,* Cholla Needles Press (2017) cynthiaandersonpoet.com

Kim Barnes, a University of Idaho Distinguished Professor Emerita and former Idaho Writer-in-Residence, was raised in the logging camps and small towns of northern Idaho. Her books have been named among the best of the year by *San Francisco Chronicle, The Seattle Times, The Washington Post,* and *The Kansas City Star.* Her novel *A Country Called Home* received the PEN Center USA Award, and her memoir *In the Wilderness* was a finalist for the Pulitzer Prize. www.kimbarnes.com

Mary Brancaccio is author of *Fierce Geometry* (2022, Get Fresh Books). Her poetry has appeared in *Naugatuck River Review, Minerva Rising, Edison Literary Review, Lake Affect Magazine* and *Adana,* among others. A Pushcart Prize nominee and an MFA in Poetry, she is included in several anthologies including *Writing the Land: Maine, Writing the Land: Northeast, Farewell to Nuclear, Welcome to Renewable Energy* and *Veils, Halos and Shackles: International Poetry on the Oppression and Empowerment of Women.*

Martin Bridge (cover artist) carries his family tradition forth as he lives, creates and teaches in Western Massachusetts. His work spans a wide range of media: Drawing, Painting, Sculpture, Theater Design, Site Specific Installations, and Performance. As an avid Permaculture designer he strives to improve his awareness of how he relates to the natural world and to live in better balance. He hopes to inspire and cultivate a greater sense of mystery and possibility.   thebridgebrothers.com

Linda Buckmaster has lived within a block of the Atlantic most of her life, growing up in Florida and living in midcoast Maine for forty years. Her poetry, essay, and fiction have appeared in over forty journals. Two of her pieces have been listed as Notable Essays in *Best American Essays*

2013 and 2020. Her hybrid memoir, *Space Heart. A Memoir in Stages*, was published by Burrow Press in 2018. Her latest hybrid is *Elemental: A Miscellany of Salt Cod and Islands* (Huntress Press 2022).

For forty years **Michael Carey** farmed 800 acres in southwest Iowa and wrote poetry and essays concerning culture and agriculture. He is a graduate of Lafayette College and the University of Iowa's Writers' Workshop. His work has been widely published in literary magazines across the United States, Great Britain and Ireland. His books of poetry include: *The Noise the Earth Makes, Honest Effort, Nishnabotna, Carpenter of Song*, and *The Holy Ground*.

Dan Close is poet and novelist living in the hills of northwestern Vermont. He is the author of a new book of poetry entitled *The Night The Moon Went Sailing*, which joins his previous book of poetry, *What The Abenaki Say About Dogs*. His novel *The Glory of the Kings* was awarded Best In Fiction for 2014 by Peace Corps Writers. His 2nd novel, *Song of Quebec*, is set in 1971 Quebec City at the height of the Quiet Revolution. He currently is a member of the Poetry Society of Vermont.

Candace R. Curran authored *Playing in Wrecks* and co-authored *Bone Cages* with Doug Anderson, John Hodgen et al. (Haley's Press). She is a founding member of word and image multimedia exhibitions, Interface I-X and Exploded View and is most interested in poetry that invites word as art. Poems have appeared in *Meat For Tea, the Valley Review, Silkworm, raW NerVZ Haiku* and *Compass Roads*. Her Elyse Wolf chapbook prize winning manuscript is forthcoming from Slate Roof Press.

Patrick Curry is a Canadian-born long-time resident of London, England. He is the author of several books on the social history of astrology, the work of J.R.R. Tolkien, and ecological philosophy. His most recent books are *Enchantment: Wonder in Modern Life* (2019) and *Art and Enchantment: How Wonder Works* (2023). He edits the online journal *The Ecological Citizen* and is a Companion of Ruskin's educational charity The Guild of St George.

Marty Espinola became interested in photography at the age of 15 and soon was developing and printing pictures in a makeshift darkroom.

Later as a school teacher he worked weekends as a newspaper and freelance photographer. Now retired, Marty enjoys pursuing his love of nature photography, mentoring local photography groups and doing workshops. lighteffects.shutterfly.com. Martyesp1@yahoo.com

Victoria Field is a writer, researcher and poetry therapist living in Canterbury, Kent, UK. She has published four collections of poetry, most recently *A Speech of Birds* (2020), and a memoir of pilgrimage and marriage, *Baggage: A Book of Leavings* (2016), both from Francis Boutle Publishers. Her doctoral studies examined narratives of transformation in pilgrimage. She is a pioneer in the UK in the use of poetry and healing.

Robert Fleming (b. 1963) is a word-artist from Lewes, Delaware, United States. Robert follows his mother as a visual artist and his grandfather as a poet. Contributing editor of Old Scratch Press Short-Form Collective. Member of the Rehoboth Beach and Horror Writers Association. Wins: 2022 San Gabriel Valley California-1 poem, 2021 Best of Mad Swirl poetry; Nominations: 2 Pushcart and 2 Best of the Net. https://www.facebook.com/robert.fleming.5030

Mireille Gansel's lyrical memoir, *Translation as Transhumance* (English translation by Ros Schwartz) contributed significantly to the field of translation studies. Her awards include: the Veu Lliure 2021 Prize (Catalan PEN); Laureate of the Great Prize of Translation Etienne Dolet-Sorbonne Université (2018); the Khoury-Ghata poetry prize; the Gérald de Nerval translation prize; an English PEN Award; a French Voices Award; and others for German and Vietnamese poet translations.

Dr. Gojmerac-Leiner is a clinically trained health care chaplain. Nature was and is the balm for processing her work. She is an avid hiker, gardener and cook. She has been a poet since adolescence while she was growing up in Pravutina, Croatia. She published her first poem in English as a high school student in Connecticut. Many years later she has many journals, both local and national, and poetic and pastoral lining her shelves, including most recently *Passager, Bethany Poets* and *Bostonia*.

Robin Lily Goldberg is an interdisciplinary artist exploring the reciprocity between ecology and creativity. Her contemplative writing illuminates interspecies collaborations and their vital contributions to ecosystem wholeness. She is an MFA candidate as well as a founding curator and co-editor of an EcoArt magazine. Her words have appeared in dozens of journals, and in 2014, Charing Cross Press published her first book, a poetry collection called *The Sound of Seeds.*

Chandra Gurung was born in a remote village in Nepal. He has a deep passion for poetry, and is active as a translator of many foreign language poems into Nepali. In 2007 he published his first poetry anthology, his second collection, *My Father's Face,* has been translated into English (2020); his third poetry collection came out in 2022. His work has been featured in many international anthologies including: *More of My Beautiful Bahrain, Snow Jewel, The Collections of Poetry and Prose series, Warscapes.com.*

Alyson Hallett is a prize-winning poet. She was recently EarthArt Fellow in the Earth Sciences department of Bristol University, collaborating with volcanologists. As well as writing for the page, her poems are carved into a city pavement and etched in library windows. Alyson curates the international poetry and public art project, The Migration Habits of Stones, which involves siting rocks with words carved into them in different countries around the world.

Cathryn Hankla is a native of Southwest Virginia who recently retired from Hollins University as professor emerita after a long career in education. She has published sixteen books of fiction, nonfiction, and poetry, among them the memoir in essays *Lost Places: on Losing and Finding Home* (2018), *Immortal Stuff: prose poems* (2023), *Not Xanadu* (2022), *Galaxies* (2017), and *Great Bear* (2016), which was a finalist for the Library of Virginia prize in poetry. www.cathrynhankla.com

Sharon Harmon has two chapbooks, *Wishbone in a Lightning Jar,* (Flutter Press) and also *Swimming with Cats,* (Autumn Light Press). She has been published in *Compass Roads, The Auroean, Silkworm, The Agape Review, The Patterson Literary Review,* and many other publications. She is a freelance writer for magazines and the author of two children's books and is working on a new chapbook, *Trailer Park Children.* Sharon resides deep in the woods of Royalston where she often finds her inspiration

James Harpur has published eight books of poetry with Anvil Press, Carcanet and Two Rivers Press, and has won a number of prizes and awards, including the UK National Poetry Competition. His debut novel, *The Pathless Country*, won the JG Farrell Award and was shortlisted for the John McGahern Prize. He lives in West Cork and is a member of Aosdána, the Irish academy of the arts.

Diana Hirst's childhood was spent in East Kent, and its changing seascapes and chalk countryside are a continual source of inspiration for her poetry. Other major influences have been word-play with her family, the houses she has lived in, finding her ancestors, and music. She was Deal and Dover Poet of the Year in 2008, and her poems have been commended in the Canterbury Festival, Suffolk and Wivenhoe competitions.

W. Luther Jett is a Maryland native and a retired special educator. His poetry has been published in numerous journals and anthologies. Luther's poem "How Many Fingers' was nominated for the 2022 Pushcart Prize. He is the author of five poetry chapbooks: *Not Quite: Poems Written in Search of My Father* (Finishing Line Press, 2015), *Our Situation* (Prolific Press, 2018), *Everyone Disappears* (Finishing Line Press, 2020), *Little Wars* (Kelsay Books, 2021) and *Watchman, What of the Night?* (CW Books, 2022)

Kathy Kremins is a retired New Jersey public school teacher. She has two chapbooks of poems, *Seamus & His Smalls* (Two Key Customs, 2023) and *Undressing the World* (Finishing Line Press, 2022). Her first full-length poetry book, *The Curve of Things* (CavanKerry Press), will be published in Spring 2024. She is the managing editor for Platform Review and part of the feminist poetry collective *Write On! Poetry Babes*.

Roger Lebovitz is a writer living in Burlington, Vermont. He has published two books, *A Guide to the Western Slope and the Outlying Areas*, and *Twenty-two Instructions for Near Survival*, both published by Fomite Press, as well as several shorter pieces in various journals. The land he lives on is only lately emerged after being underwater or under ice for most of the past fifty thousand years.

DJ Lee is a writer, scholar, and artist with forty lyrical essays and prose poems in magazines and anthologies, and books: *Remote: Finding Home in the Bitterroots* (Oregon State, 2020), and *The Edge Is What We Have: Awe and Wonder in a Dimming World* (Oregon State, forthcoming 2024). A hand papermaker and photographer, Lee often combines image and text. She has published eight scholarly books on wilderness, 19th-century literature, and oral history. She teaches at Washington State University.

Angela Leighton is Senior Research Fellow at Trinity College, Cambridge. As well as many works of literary criticism, including *Hearing Things: The Work of Sound in Literature* (Harvard 2018), she has published five volumes of poetry, most recently *One, Two* (Carcanet 2021). Her next volume, *Something, I Forget*, is forthcoming in October 2023.

Earl Livings is a poet and fiction writer who has been widely published in Australia and overseas. His writing focuses on science, history, nature, mythology and the sacred. He has published two poetry collections, *Libation* (Ginninderra Press) and *Further than Night*, (Bystander Press), and a fantasy verse novel, *The Silence Inside the World* (Peggy Bright Books, 2023). Earl lives in Melbourne with his wife and their ever-growing stacks of books.

Jesse LoVasco, (she/her) is a poet, visual artist and herbalist residing in unceded land of both Anishnabe in Michigan and Abenaki in Vermont. She studied poetry at Vermont College. Her book *Native* was published in 2020, and she was a participating fellow of NatureCulture's Writing the Land Project, with poems in the anthology *Windblown I*, as well as a yearly contributor and facilitator for PoemCity in Montpelier, VT.

Janet MacFadyen is author of five poetry books, with a new collection forthcoming from Salmon Poetry. Honors include a Massachusetts Cultural Council grant, a Fine Arts Work Center fellowship, and Pushcart, Forward, and Best of the Net nominations. Her poetry appears in *Crannóg, Naugatuck River Review, Osiris, Soul-Lit*, and *Scientific American*. She has a degree in geology, is the managing editor of Slate Roof Press, and lives in the forests of western Massachusetts.

Susan Marsh lives in Jackson, Wyoming, where she is grateful to find wild nature, from forests to feeder birds, at her door. Her books include an award-winning novel, *War Creek*, ten non-fiction books, and a poetry chapbook, *This Earth Has Been Too Generous*. She writes a column "Back to Nature" for Mountain Journal.

Rodger Martin's *For All The Tea in Zhōngguó*, 2019, follows *The Battlefield Guide*, and the selection of *The Blue Moon Series* by Small Press Review as one of its bi-monthly picks of the year. He's received an Appalachia award for poetry, NHSCA's award for fiction, and fellowships from the National Endowment for the Humanities.

Caitlín Matthews is the author of over 80 books, including *Celtic Devotional* and *The Lost Book of the Grail*. Her poetry was published in *Poetry London* by Tambimuttu, and her first collection, *Search for Rhiannon* appeared in 1981. Internationally known for her work on the mythic and ancestral traditions of Britain and Ireland, Caitlín is a co-founder of the Foundation for Inspirational and Oracular Studies (FÍOS). She has a shamanic healing practice in Oxford. www.hallowquest.org.uk

John Matthews is an independent poet and scholar living in Oxford. He published his first book in 1980 and has since gone on to publish over a hundred titles on Myth, Folklore, and ancient traditions. He has made a lifetime study of every aspect of the Arthurian legends, from its origins to modern retellings, and wrote a bestselling work on the history of piracy.

Libby Maxey is a senior editor at Literary Mama and a winner of the 2021 Princemere Poetry Prize. Her work has appeared in *Emrys, The Maynard, Crannóg Magazine* and elsewhere, and her chapbook, *Kairos* (2019), won Finishing Line Press's New Women's Voices contest. Her nonliterary activities include singing classical repertoire and mothering sons. She lives with her family in Western Massachusetts.

Poet, editor, and educator **Dana Maya** is from "Greater Mexico"—a space transcending geopolitical, cultural, linguistic, & creative borders. She attended Vassar College & the University of Texas at Austin, with an orientation in Chicanx, Queer, & Race, and has taught in colleges, K12, & community organizations. Dana collaborates with artists on projects for social change. Her writing has won awards & appears in anthologies, journals, buses, stages, museums, memorial sites, & other spaces.

Tina Meyer grew up in the Connecticut River Valley and has lived here most of her life. She is semi-retired and moved to Florence, Massachusetts a few years ago. She spends much time familiarizing herself with the abundant land trusts and reservations in the area. She is an avid hiker of trails and walker of woods. She has been a poet since the inception of her spirit.

Kathryn Millar has lived a wild and adventurous life. She is honored to be writing for the land and she loves to listen to mother Earth! She is a teacher, writer, fiber artist, farmer, traveler and more. Living every day with awe and gratitude.

Claire Millikin is the author of nine collections of poetry, and a 2021 recipient of the Maine Literary Award. Millikin's newest books are *Dolls* (2Leaf Press 2021), *Transitional Objects* (Unicorn Press 2022), and *Elegiaca Americana* (Littoral Books 2022), a book of elegies for America. Millikin lives in coastal Maine and teaches American Studies at Bates College and art history for the University of Maine.

Dr. Gwyn R. C. Moses is an Educator residing in Richmond, Virginia. She is a contributing Poet of *Writing The Land: Windblown I*. She is featured in *Virginia Bards Central Review Poetry Anthology, 2022 & 2019*. Poetic collections include *SHE: Fully Hydrated, Olive Grey, Down by The Riverside*, and *Reflections: Connect with God*. Dr. Moses' Podcast is 'Nature Amends.' When she is not writing, Author Moses muses in nature and the arts.

Carolyn Oulton is Professor of Victorian Literature and Director of the International Centre for Victorian Women Writers at Canterbury Christ Church University. She teaches on the Creative and Professional Writing BA and is Co-Lead for the Kent digital heritage project https://kent-maps.online/ in collaboration with JSTOR Labs. Her most recent poetry collection is *Accidental Fruit* (Worple).

Dr. Sonia Overall is a writer, psychogeographer and academic living in East Kent. Her published work includes novels, poetry, short stories, academic articles and features, many of which explore place, aspects of the weird and experimental forms. Her latest books are a hybrid memoir *Heavy Time* (2021) and a novel, *Eden* (2022). Sonia is currently a Senior Lecturer at Canterbury Christ Church University, where she runs the MA in Creative Writing. www.soniaoverall.net Twitter @soniaoverall

Maria Perez is an 20 year old writer, poet, and artist who grew up in the Bronx and now lives on Staten Island. Maria attends Kingsborough Community College pursuing her dream of becoming a teacher. She is published in the Young Writers USA *Imagine,* and *Writing the Land: Foodways and Social Justice.* She is working on a self-published autobiography titled *We Will Love Again*, available through Substack: nymphaeariaa.substack.com

Charles A. Perrone was born in the Empire State of New York, grew up in the Golden State of California, last studied in the Lone Star State of Texas, and completed an academic career in the Sunshine State of Florida. He returned to the Central Coast of California after a forty year absence because it is a great place to be, think, write, play music, do radio, and keep on truckin'.

Katherine Pierpoint was raised in Northamptonshire, UK. She has a deep love of the natural realm; its own poetry and transformative power, as we honor the land. Qualified as an energy healer, she spends her time between Glastonbury and Canterbury. She was *Sunday Times* Young Writer of the Year, 1996. Her poetry collection, *Truffle Beds* (Faber, 1995) won a Somerset Maugham Award, and was shortlisted for the T.S. Eliot prize. Her poem 'The egg-slicer' won the Troubadour International prize.

Patrice Pinette is inspired by creative collaborations between poets, artists and musicians. She facilitates NH Humanities Connections programs and teaches in Antioch New England's Waldorf Education program. She holds an MFA in Writing from VCFA, and her poems have appeared in *Pensive Journal; Poets Touchstone, Inflectionist Review; Allegro Poetry Magazine; Writing the Land; The Hampden-Sydney Poetry Review; Poetica Magazine; Snapdragon Journal of Art and Healing,* and elsewhere.

Sean Prentiss is the author of *Finding Abbey: the Search for Edward Abbey and His Hidden Desert Grave*, which won the National Outdoor Book Award, and *Crosscut: Poems*. He co-wrote two textbooks, *Environmental and Nature Writing* and *Advanced Creative Nonfiction*. Prentiss is co-editor of *The Science of Story: The Brain Behind Creative Nonfiction*. He and his family live on a small lake in northern Vermont, and he serves as an associate professor at Norwich University.

Suzanne S. Rancourt, Abenaki/Huron, Quebecois, Scottish descent, USMC and Army Veteran: author of NU Press & Native Writers' Circle of the Americas First Book Award, *Billboard in the Clouds;* Poetry of Modern Conflict award-winner *murmurs at the gate* (Unsolicited Press 2019); *Old Stones, New Roads* (MSR, 2021); *Songs of Archilochus* (Unsolicited Press, 2023). She's a multimodal EXAT, CASAC, w/ degrees in psych., writing, Aikido, Iaido & *Writing the Land* Fellow. www.expressive-arts.com

Shann Ray teaches at Gonzaga University and Stanford University. A National Endowment for the Arts Fellow, he has been a visiting scholar in Africa, Asia, Europe, and the Americas. Ray is an American Book Award winner, three-time High Plains Book Award winner, Bread Loaf Fellow, and Bakeless Prize winner. His work includes *Blood Fire Vapor Smoke* and *The Souls of Others*, and has been featured in *Poetry, Esquire, McSweeney's* and *Narrative*.

Elaine Reardon lives and writes next to a forest stream in Western Massachusetts. Her first chapbook, *The Heart is a Nursery For Hope*, won first honors from Flutter Press in 2016. Her second chapbook, *Look Behind You*, was published in late 2019. Her writing is published in a variety of journals and anthologies.   elainereardon.wordpress.com.

Julie Ross is a retired Consultant Clinical Psychologist, and Psychoanalytic Psychotherapist. Her career was spent as a senior NHS clinical leader with responsibility for professional standards and quality of care. Since then, she has completed a Masters degree in Myth, Cosmology, and the Sacred at Canterbury Christchurch University. She has many years' experience in the Western Mysteries, deeply interested in the sacred land and the faery tradition in Tolkien's legendarium.

Heidi Seaborn is Executive Editor of *The Adroit Journal* and winner of the 2022 *The Missouri Review* Jeffrey E. Smith Editor's Prize in Poetry. She is the author of three award-winning books/chapbooks of poetry: *An Insomniac's Slumber Party with Marilyn Monroe, Give a Girl Chaos,* and *Bite Marks.* Recent work in *Blackbird, Beloit, Brevity, Copper Nickel, diode, Financial Times of London, Poetry Northwest, Penn Review, The Slowdown* and elsewhere. Heidi holds an MFA from NYU. heidiseabornpoet.com

Lynne Shapiro is the author of two chapbooks, *Gala* (Solitude Hill Press) and *To Set Right* (Wordtech Communications). She co-edited *Dark as A Hazel Eye: Coffee and Chocolate Poems* (Ragged Sky Press) and has been published in such anthologies as *Decomposition: An Anthology of Fungi Inspired Poems* (Lost Horse Press) and *Welcome to the Resistance, Poetry as Protest* (Stockton University Press). Lynne has been a poet-in-residence in England, Morocco, and Spain. lynneshapiropoet.com.

Joan Seliger Sidney is Writer-in-Residence at the University of Connecticut's Center for Judaic Studies and Contemporary Jewish Life. She authored *Body of Diminishing Motion: Poems and a Memoir* (an Eric Hoffer Legacy Finalist, CavanKerry), *Bereft and Blessed* (AntrimHouse), and *The Way the Past Comes Back* (The Kutenai Press). Poems from *Soul House* have appeared in *The Common, Asymptote, New Poetry in Translation* and were nominated for a Pushcart Prize.

Yehudit Silverman, M.A. R-DMT, RDT Former Chair, Department of Creative Arts Therapies, Concordia University, Montreal, is the author of several articles, OpEds, and recent book, *The Story Within – myth and fairy tale in therapy.* An award-winning documentary filmmaker, she received several federal and provincial grants to work on issues around suicide, and interfaith arts dialogue. She writes poetry, leads creative lifecycle rituals and presentations internationally. www.yehuditsilverman.com

A Franco-American poet, **Jeri Theriault** grew up in Maine. Her teaching career spanned 34 years. She is the author of *Radost, my red* and *Self-Portrait as Homestead,* and the editor of *WAIT: Poems from the Pandemic.* Her poems and reviews appear in *The Rumpus, The Texas Review, The Atlanta Review, Asheville Poetry Review, Plume,* and many others. Recent awards include the 2023 Maine Arts Commission Literary Arts Fellowship, the 2023 Monson Arts Fellowship and the 2022 NORward Prize.

Tammi J Truax has worked as a teacher in a variety of settings, co-founded The Prickly Pear Poetry Project, was editor of *The Poet's Tale; Lady Wentworth* (2013), and author of *Broken Buckets* (2013) and a YA novel in verse *For to See the Elephant* (2019). Her poetry has appeared in 15 anthologies, and in journals, newspapers, and online. She was the Maine Beat Poet Laureate for two years and the Portsmouth (NH) Poet Laureate for three years, with a project featured in *The New York Times.*

Dorinda Wegener is a Perianesthesia Certified Registered Nurse in Richmond, VA. She has work forthcoming in *Hayden's Ferry Review*, as well as poems published in many journals, including *The Antioch Review, THRUSH, Indiana Review, Hotel Amerika*, and *Berkeley Poetry Review.* Her first full length book, *Four Fields*, is forthcoming from Trio House Press in 2024.

Meg Weston is a poet, non-fiction writer, and photographer with passion for the geological processes that shape the earth and the stories that shape our lives. She has an MFA from Lesley University. As Co-founder of The Poets Corner www.thepoetscorner.org, and the Camden Festival of Poetry, Meg actively supports the poetry community. www.volcanoes.com Her forthcoming poetry collection, *Magma Intrusions*, is due out in September 2023.

Robert Wrigley was born in Illinois and has lived in Montana, Washington, Oregon, and mostly Idaho. He has published eleven books of poems and one collection of essays, *Nemerov's Door.* A new book of poems, *The True Account of Myself as a Bird*, was published by Penguin in June, 2022. A former Idaho Writer-in-Residence, he is the recipient of two NEA Fellowships and a Guggenheim Foundation Fellowship. He lives in the woods near Moscow, Idaho www.robertwrigley.com

Yuan Hongri (born 1962) is a renowned Chinese mystic, poet, and philosopher whose work explores themes of prehistoric and future civilization. He has been published in the UK, USA, India, New Zealand, Canada, and Nigeria in *Poet's Espresso Review, Orbis, Tipton Poetry Journal, Harbinger Asylum, The Stray Branch, Pinyon Review, Taj Mahal Review, Madswirl, Shot Glass Journal,* and other e-zines, anthologies, and journals. His best known works are "Platinum City" and "Golden Giant."

Yuanbing Zhang (b. 1974), is Mr. Yuan Hongri's assistant and translator. He himself is a Chinese poet and translator, and works in a Middle School, Yanzhou District, Jining City, Shandong Province China. He can be contacted through his email 3112362909@qq.com

About the Editor, Dr. Simon Richard Wilson

Simon Richard Wilson is a Senior Lecturer in the Faculty of Arts, Humanities and Education at Canterbury Christ Church University (UK), and a member of the Institute for Orthodox Christian Studies at Cambridge (UK). He has a special interest in landscape, co-creation, love of learning, the theology of the Eastern Orthodox Church, and the true nature of sustainability.

About the Foreword Author, Dr. Joel Berger

My fascination with biodiversity began in LA (California) where I grew up. I traded body surfing for desert and mountain explorations, and melded that pursuit into serious science. But, I also soon realized that if we did not do more than just science we'd not have species and important biological interactions from which to enhance our understanding of a diverse and brilliant planet. I've concentrated on animals larger than a bread box – both iconic endangered species and those lesser known. Among these have been black rhinos and wild yaks, Patagonia's huemul, and saiga in Mongolia's Gobi Desert. Although I've targeted extreme

spots – described in my Geographical pursuits – including the edges of the planet, I ask questions about climate and environmental change, migration and connectivity, and, most recently, how our burgeoning passion for play and our travel footprints affect species at a local scale. In my soul, I know the important issue is how to engage science at levels that not only inform but improve visibility and result in change.

www.ingramcontent.com/pod-product-compliance
Lightning Source LLC
Chambersburg PA
CBHW030221140626
46545CB00011B/533